PAST LIFETIMES:

KEYS FOR CHANGE

Annie O'Grady

Sally Milner Publishing

First published in 1997 by
Sally Milner Publishing Pty Ltd
RMB 54 Burra Road
Burra Creek
NSW Australia 2620

© Annie O'Grady, 1997

Cover design by ANU Graphics, Canberra
Cover photograph from the Australian Picture Library
Printing by National Capital Printing, Canberra
Typesetting by Maureen Miller

National Library of Australia Cataloguing-in-Publication:

O'Grady, Annie.
Past lifetimes: keys for change

Bibliography.
ISBN 1 86351 170 9

1. Reincarnation. 2. Reincarnation therapy. I. Title.

133.90135

*To be shaken out of the ruts of ordinary perception ...
is an experience of inestimable value to everyone.*

Aldous Huxley

*The important lesson is that people must be ... educated
about the crucial interrelationships between their bodies,
minds, emotions and spiritual energies.*

Dr Richard Gerber

*We are not just highly evolved animals with biological
computers embedded inside our skulls; we are also fields
of consciousness without limits, transcending time,
space, matter and lineal causality.*

Dr Stanislav Grof

*A man who never changes his opinions is like
standing water, and breeds reptiles of the mind.*

William Blake

ACKNOWLEDGEMENTS

I thank all those courageous adventurers who have journeyed with me beyond the ordinary, to their intensely personal lands of discovery and self-healing. Permission to tell their stories is appreciated.

And I thank my many teachers. I also learn much from those whom I guide and teach, as this book shows. It is a joy to pass on learning.

Names and some personal details of past-lifetime travellers have been changed to protect their privacy. In the interests of brevity, a few cases are composites.

DISCLAIMER
Past lifetimes counselling is not intended to replace physical treatment for disease. If you have health problems, seek medical advice.

DEDICATION

To Shaunna, Chris and Savannah, with love

CONTENTS

TALES FROM AN ARMCHAIR TRAVELLER

Suppose you settle into your own time machine – your reclining armchair. You could be feeling meditative, or about to listen to a guiding tape. You focus the controls (your mind and inner senses), release the brakes (your tensions) and gently waft into space-time orbit.

Thousands of years away and somewhere else, you may find yourself beside a cooking fire in a Stone Age encampment. Strange primitive people grimace at you, grunt and yammer, reach towards you – handing you a morsel of roast mammoth. You may tremble with amazement and delight, especially thrilled because you arrived here safely, with all your brain cells intact and your return flight reserved.

Or perhaps you yearn for a more romantic mode of travel? That magic Oriental carpet in your living room, for example. If you lie on it and relax, can this familiar carpet fly you softly through the haze of centuries, to rendezvous with your favourite period of history?

Will you float down on to a sweet-smelling meadow outside a mediaeval castle at carnival time? Could you find yourself mingling with a rough country crowd of long ago? You might glimpse the scarlet tights of tumblers, dance to the tinkle of jester's bells and the thump of hide drums, catch an elbow in the ribs from a strolling nobleman, reel with pleasure at the aroma of a basket of fresh rosy apples in the days when apples were apples.

Yet you arrive back home in time for dinner enriched by your experience, your personal horizons expanded. Still hearing the growls of bears performing to laughter that echoes over six centuries, still smelling smoke from logs that burned to ash aeons ago.

And over your bowl of packaged soup you wonder if perhaps, in this life, you could learn to play the flute or the drums, or go out dancing for a change. Or get out into the countryside more, and sit with friends around a campfire.

They say travel broadens the mind.

PART ONE:

WHAT'S IT ALL ABOUT?

Chapter One

What is Past Lifetimes Counselling?

Past lifetimes counselling is a guiding skill. It enables people to experience impressions that seem to be from their past lifetimes — and enables them to utilise these discoveries, to create change for the better in the present.

It is a unique approach to personal growth and self-improvement. Strange but true, say its admirers, that exploring the past in this way leads us to live more fully in the present moment. As a self-transformation consultant, I have found that past-life work does this so effectively that I have specialised in it for 13 years.

People take past lifetime journeys because of any present problem or limitation. Even when the motive is, 'I just want to find out if I've lived before', the urge is to heal ignorance of our deeper dimensions, to discover more of our wider nature and potentials.

This book will show that we don't have to carry burdens from other lifetimes we may have lived. The stories we discover from history and pre-history can become keys for change — tools for resolving and releasing deep-seated barriers that prevent us from going forward in our present life. They can also liberate intense feelings of joy and inspiration into our present lives.

The past is not dead and gone until we have finished with it. Psychologists agree that traces of the past in this life are active and visible in our present feelings, attitudes, thoughts, conversations and behaviour. Psychological problems rooted in the past remain alive in the present until we resolve old issues, or wear them out over years. Issues personal to us appear in different guises in our past-life stories. This suggests we bring unfinished business into this life — giving ourselves another chance to resolve it.

Invariably this psycho-spiritual path brings new understandings, not only of ourselves but also of other people, and even of the human condition. But in many cases it has done more. Countless people report that some metaphysical resonance from inner work through past lifetime stories has freed up situations they are in now.

Past-life work is practical mysticism. Its concern is valuable change for the living individual. We might say it mysteriously enables other people to come to life within us, to assist us now. Through it people have found life direction, lost crippling fears, dissolved confusion, unravelled bitter conflicts, improved their physical wellbeing, stimulated creativity, contacted dormant abilities. Many have deepened the bonds of love through tracing their soul journeys with people they love now.

How do people recall their past lifetimes? Read on. You may be startled to find that such recall is available to many people through a simple breathing practice — whether they believe in reincarnation or not. I outline this, and some of my other methods, in the Appendix.

All those undertaking a past lifetime journey, whether of minutes or hours, seem to be exploring the nature of reality more deeply than some others do in a lifetime. Their range of experiences requires the practitioner to go way beyond conventional limits — to accompany clients into unknown realms, free of preconception and prejudice. In past lifetimes counselling, the learning is on both sides.

Case study one
Derek, a businessman at a breath therapy workshop, lies on a mattress while music plays, closes his eyes, and begins to breathe in a steady rhythm. Minutes later he laughs. He keeps on laughing. People around start laughing too, not knowing why. He laughs for about ten minutes.

Later he says, 'I waited 400 years for that laugh. Those jerks thought they'd killed me. But here I am alive.' He laughs again. Through a simple breathing practice, Derek has spontaneously recalled being lynched in a previous life — not usually a laughing matter.

Case study two
Josephine has a severe petrochemical allergy that leaves her nauseated and in pain for some days if she smells a felt-tipped pen.

4

Voluntarily, Josephine re-experiences an ancient drowning. She feels she is a woman falling into a river during an earthquake she associates with the Mediterranean area. I support her as for a minute or two she struggles and chokes, appearing to be trapped between swallowing water and breathing in the sulphurous fumes above the river surface.

Afterwards, she holds a felt-tipped pen to her nose. She can smell it, but that's all. She has instantly lost that allergy sensitivity. The loss proves permanent. It seems as though the smell had been reminding her unconsciously of a terror experienced by someone else, an event not fully faced because of death. Mysteriously, this experience had connected with her current life through illness, in a small Australian city that has never had a devastating earthquake.

Case study three
Alan is a commercial artist. Recent retrenchment has brought a disastrous slump in his self-esteem. He dreams of a horizontal volcano spitting lumps of fire.

As he re-enters the dream in my consulting room, a dream character reminds him of his childhood nightmares of grotesque biplanes. Then he feels he is an adult piloting a biplane, a young German pilot in World War I. When his plane crashes in enemy fire the pilot dies in confusion, feeling he has failed by somehow causing the crash.

During the dream work, Alan realises that artillery fire caused the crash — that the dream volcano spitting flames sideways was a coded message of gunfire. In a profound visualisation, the depressed artist counsels his past self, the young German, that he is not a failure.

The experience so improves Alan's self-confidence that he later describes it as 'magic'. He opens up to new possibilities. He is also intrigued that in this life he is Australian — and his past German self was, within the same century, a former enemy of Australia. (Until the unifying dream work, had one part of him been at war with another?)

ARE THEY MAKING IT UP?
Inevitably the question emerges: are these life stories from the mind fiction or non-fiction? Have we lived before, or are we making it up?

5

Reincarnation is the concept that Earth is a school for the evolution of consciousness, for the human race and perhaps also for other life forms. Adherents believe our purpose in living in the form of a series of humans is to undertake multiple lessons in reaching our highest potential as developing conscious beings.

Because of their personal experiences of past-life recall, countless Westerners claim that yes, we do lead a series of lives in different bodies on Earth. They say that at least some of those lives directly influence us now, for better or for worse. They say that past lifetime exploration simply extends the scope of memory to include these lives.

While reincarnation is an obvious explanation of living stories hiding in our consciousness, it is not the only one. Other people prefer to regard these as 'mind metaphors', or inner movies, of a similar order to dreams. The life stories, they say, are gifts our psyche creates to illuminate hidden facets of our present existence so that we may improve our quality of life.

Both approaches attempt to explain a phenomenon that is becoming more visible in Western society every day, as more people experience and investigate it. This is a surprising human ability to receive undirected inner impressions that add up to life stories of other people, or even of animals, no matter where we enter these stories, nor how quickly we jump around in time. Inherent in these discoveries is potential for self-healing in the present.

Discovery of this human ability prompted New York Jungian psychotherapist Dr Roger Woolger, initially a sceptic, to comment that this valuable new realm of the psyche, largely unsuspected in the West until recently, may even lead to a radical re-evaluation of human personality. Other distinguished practioner/researchers agree.

STORIES AS SYMBOLS

Past-life work does not need belief. Its stories can be seen as symbols. Symbols are the language of the unconscious mind. Symbols may present themselves to us as physical shapes, or dreams, or stories. For example, fairy tales, myths and legends often deal with issues of daily life through symbols. The Swiss consciousness research pioneer, Dr Carl Jung, wrote that as our minds explore symbols, we are led beyond the confines of reason alone.

Understanding our dreams as symbols, through learning their special language, allows them to highlight secrets about ourselves that need our conscious attention. We do not demand that dreams be proven true before they are used as healing agents, as signposts to self-awareness. So we do not need to demand that past-life stories and their details be proven true — although many have been, partly or wholly.

Because stories are easier to understand than dreams, past lifetimes represent a simpler code. Viewing past-life impressions as a different kind of dream allows reincarnation doubters to take advantage of the 'recall' process.

A sceptic was open-minded enough to take an inner journey at one of my workshops. Afterwards he was excited because his arm was hurting. (It's more usual that people arrive with pain and leave without it!) His excitement was because in his past-life recall a lion had bitten off that arm. His arm was showing him evidence of the mind/body connection that is the basis of holistic healthcare systems. The pain did not persist, but his fascination with inner dimensions did.

Growing international documentation of past lifetimes recall suggests that humans are walking libraries or movie houses. It is beginning to look as though perhaps we all are able to revive unsuspected fragments of awareness that add up to life stories of other people. And that the act of remembering alone may begin to unlock present secrets of mind and matter.

DEPTHS OF THE PSYCHE

For myself, after witnessing hundreds of recalls of other lifetimes and their beneficial effects on present experience, I am intrigued by the many levels of what emerges, affecting mind, emotions, body, spirit. My own inner discoveries of past lifetimes have been varied and powerful. As well as accelerating my growth, they have given me tolerance for the strange findings of other people in non-ordinary states of awareness.

Some modern consciousness researchers, such as Czech-born Dr Stanislav Grof, an American psychiatrist, have painstakingly observed and mapped unusual awarenesses that people, including themselves, actually experience, in altered states of consciousness. Much of this uncovered material lies beyond normal conventions. Rather than trying to fit non-ordinary perceptions into old theories of what is or isn't to be labelled crazy, such researchers go far beyond traditional psychiatric theories that consider mystical events as pathological.

The new cartography of the psyche, or map of consciousness, delineated by Dr Grof from the sum of thousands of people's experiences, vastly expands the boundaries of what a human being may experience while sane (see his book, *The Adventure of Self Discovery*).

In the United States in the 1960s, Dr Grof was a co-founder of the transpersonal psychology movement, which has been described as the umbrella under which science meets mysticism. It is the fourth major psychological approach, after behaviourism, psychoanalysis, and humanistic psychology. This approach recognises the existence and values of certain dimensions of non-ordinary experience. The human urge towards spirituality and the transcendental is so powerful, according to Dr Grof, that its denial or repression seriously distorts both individuals and societies.

Transpersonal psychology sees mystical experiences not only as genuine personal events, but also as vital ingredients in the ongoing evolutionary processes of human development. One of these dimensions can be past lifetimes recall.

Old boundaries between psychic and normal are publicly melting in many directions, as new books, films, videos and television programs demonstrate. The growing international popularity of past lifetimes literature shows the scope of new interest. The numbers alone of inner explorers constitute a phenomenon.

A poll of the U.S. population reported in *Newsweek* in 1994 showed that 20% of Americans believe they had a revelation from God in the previous year, 13% reported having seen or sensed the presence of an angel, 33% had had a religious or mystical experience, and 58% felt a need to experience spiritual growth.

In the last decade, researchers in conventional scientific disciplines have increasingly extended into parapsychology.

Why do we need to contact past lives? We don't need to — unless they contact us spontaneously. Yet exploration is a precious gift we can give ourselves. Rewards can mean renewal in some blocked area of life now, whether or not we've been aware of the stress. And when we consciously feel stressed through blockage, change, trauma or deficiency, we can tap inner resources that seem to involve our own soul history. While this approach is not a blanket remedy for everyone's ills, as one of my students said, 'What a lovely way to heal!'

HOW DOES 'RECALL' HAPPEN?

A great deal of spontaneous past lifetime memory is now being reported. (Even invited impressions in past lifetimes mode come to us spontaneously, unless we're revisiting scenes contacted earlier.) Such memories can surface unexpectedly in sessions of various kinds of therapies, even if neither client nor practitioner believes in reincarnation. Many a masseur working on a cramped muscle has been startled to hear a client say something like, 'I feel as though I'm riding a horse, running away, galloping over a cliff.' For the client, tears or body shakes may follow, as trapped emotions release. This can be initially upsetting but the present relevance of the emotions or situation is usually obvious.

Other triggers for past-life recall may be places, people, movies, music, tastes, smells, pictures or symbols. Or you may just be cleaning your teeth, and suddenly you're smelling the sweat and fear of horses and men in battle, you're breathing hot dust — and you feel you are a soldier on the banks of the River Tigris, slashing your way with a sword through screaming enemy hordes.

The reason for apparently inexplicable recall may be that one of your emotional patterns is overstressed. Your current conflict with your boss may feel just like the old conflict with the enemy commander. If you suffered or died in that past lifetime sequence, your boss's anger may arouse in you feelings of dread quite out of proportion to the present situation.

When recall is intentional, regression— the act of 'going back' in consciousness — is usually done while reclining with eyes closed. With reputable past lifetimes practitioners, the impressions arise without leading questions from the guide and usually without preconceived ideas of story content. I guide people to focus initially on a particular purpose for their journey, and the ensuing story unfolds in line with this, often in unexpected ways.

In regression we are not so much story-tellers as story-dwellers. We temporarily dwell in the lives of people who have

9

lived at any time, in any place on the globe. To label regression as mere mind tripping is to ignore the full dimensions of the direct experience.

We can live through past selves' lives in both broad sweep and intimate detail, touching their feelings, thoughts, attitudes, actions, physical experiences, dreams, visions, expectations, pleasures, pain and subtle emotional shifts. And so, while the story is unfolding on the screen of our inner awareness, we can identify with these strangers, who quickly become more familiar. Although we may observe past events as though viewing a movie, we can also have deeper experiences pulling us into unexpected body sensations and strong emotions.

Impressions, or flashes of recall, are how we remember our past in any life. Present parents? 'I remember them happy, in love, dancing around the kitchen', 'I remember my mother giving me the most beautiful smile I'll remember all my life', 'I mostly remember Mum at the sink, singing', 'I remember so many painful times when my family pretended something was not happening — no wonder I became an actor.'

Sometimes memories mingle: 'When my mother was my husband in another life, he'd get a special look in his eyes when I crossed him. I see that look today, there's something in her eyes.'

With our inner senses, we might hear, in regression, the breathing of a past self, stare at the white whiskers of a long-dead cat, sense personal details strange to us ('I'm a peasant, I feel hair growing in my nose'). A slim woman says, 'My breasts feel really large.' A slim man says, 'My body feels so fat I'm overflowing this chair.' A man says, 'I can't believe this, I feel I have the breasts of a woman.' Even smells from history flash into the now — baking bread, camel dung, sweat odours from vanished bodies, overwhelming sweetness from an ancient flower garden. A few words can be poignant: 'I buried Dodie in her lace hat, all the villagers were there.' Someone else says, 'I see winter-thin cattle.' A soldier in a muddy World War 1 trench says, 'I came for the glory, but there's no glory in it.'

A story can bring surprises that cause wonder. A past self in the northern hemisphere sees a night sky the present self in the southern hemisphere has never seen; divulges detailed information quite foreign to the present self; speaks in a strange way or even in strange words. A musically unskilled woman feels as though she is a master musician, whose profound tearful response while playing the violin is, 'The universe is coming in through my heart and out through the notes.'

Most people tell past-life stories to their regression guides with an economy of words that shows each of us at heart is a natural storyteller. Stories are vibrantly presented with the freshness of immediacy. 'I'm running on a beach ... I'm wearing some sort of silk gown... the sun's warm... I smell the sea, it's calm... I'm happy...' The listener can almost hear the soft wash of wavelets. When the traveller's voice later goes hoarse, telling of a throat injury, the gaze leaps to the throat. (And sometimes relevant marks do appear on the body, as stress releases.)

IMPRESSIONS CLOSE TO US

The changing face of past lifetimes exploration shows us that many memories are not only close to the surface, but actually are alive in our words, attitudes, feelings and behaviour. Dr Woolger asks clients after regression, 'Do you know that person (past self)?' 'Oh, yes,' they usually respond, 'I've often felt like that.'

It seems that we have done our learning in varied ways. Squire, teacher, moneylender or hunter — as we work with these characters and get to understand them, we discover that all our past selves are ultimately our friends. Just as dream work demonstrates that every dream — even a 'bad' dream — carries a healing message at its core, so even past selves we don't approve of bring us denied parts of ourselves for healing and new joys.

Until other-life journeys emerge piece by piece, we are not usually aware we are carrying them, and in many cases they involve events we do not consciously wish to know. Stories may be simple and pleasant, perhaps the life of a shepherd, or a happy *hausfrau*. They may be more complex, perhaps a Scottish child victimised by vicious clan politics, or an outspoken knight put to agonising trial by his peers. Stories may even be horrendous — of World War II concentration camp victims, or inmates of secret establishments for medical experimentation. The stories can tell of foolish behaviour, of pain, longing, courageous action, desperation, ecstasy, contentment — the whole spectrum of human life.

One person's recall of lifetimes may span from the ordinary — in a variety of cultures, places and times — to the extraordinary. The experiences may be mundane, or may elicit awe at unsuspected beauty and grandeur, or even mystic bliss. Experiencing past lifetime stories can intrigue, delight, confuse, amaze, sadden or frighten us. They may bring glimpses of truth through such different lenses on human life as a peasant outlook, or the viewpoint of scientist, artist, soldier; or a quality of life belonging to a handicapped individual, or to a tribal person. (A bonus for the practitioner is that listening to so many travellers' tales is like research in oral history. I have heard described, for example, the tools of an ancient Egyptian dentist, details of a plot to kill Hitler, a secret ritual of a persecuted religion, and more.)

FEARS CAN BLOCK IMPRESSIONS

Explorers may block experience in a session through conscious or unconscious fear of what they might find. Their own discoveries may threaten cherished beliefs about how life works, or may be of shocking events. One of my solutions for blocks is an initial session of breathwork (see Appendix) to reduce the general stress load, perhaps unsuspected, of accumulated fears, confusion and exhaustion from struggling with life.

Fears may follow spontaneous past lifetimes recall. For some people spontaneous memory is precious and welcome. Others have no idea what is happening and become distraught. Other people recognise past lifetimes but are upset by them. Here the need is for at least a sympathetic hearing from a friend, or a therapist who can reassure them that countless people have safely experienced such impressions.

Because reincarnation has not been part of mainstream Western thinking, spontaneous flashes have led many people to wonder if they were going mad. Even if they felt sane, the possibility that others would think them mad was — and in some places still is — a real threat.

A 16-year-old girl, alone in her room, was suddenly flooded with vivid impressions of someone else's life. She felt as though she were a person in a civilisation which ended 2000 years ago. The memories bursting into her awareness involved sight, sound and smell, and they would not stop. In terror, the girl ran around the room with her hands over her ears, trying to shut them out, but they kept coming, over months. She found no-one to safely confide in for 20 years.

What can you do if you are anxious about flashes of memories you don't understand?

In some areas, past lifetime counsellors and therapists have phone book listings. Some psychiatrists, psychologists and other therapists include past-life work in their practices. It is wise to seek personal referrals, rather than risk an unsympathetic response.

Occasionally professional help is needed if a person appears to be stuck in the mentality of a single past lifetime. This may occur from spontaneous recall, to someone without a strong sense of his or her present individuality. It does not occur from professional regression, where completion and grounding are among a practitioner's major concerns.

Specialised practitioners have many other ways of providing support, in clarifying past and present events, and encouraging new constructive energies to flow. They understand that upset is often opportunity, a healing crisis. Properly viewed, a past lifetime story invariably connects to the present lifetime, and brings important messages. As we integrate the changes, the story itself drops behind us, finally to become just another memory we may, or may not, think of again.

People often choose professional guidance in past-life work in order to both contact, and make use of, far memories. Performing personal archaeology used to be seen as the task of a specialist using deep hypnosis, because the domain of past lifetimes was assumed to be deeply buried in consciousness. Yet in the last 20 years, a new climate of self-exploration has shown that hypnosis is often not necessary.

While such memories are rooted in the depths of our characters, they are actually readily accessible to many. We can, and do, experience two time-worlds at once through simple means, such as meditation (see Appendix). Impression flow may be stimulated through discussing past lifetimes, reading books on reincarnation, or listening to guided meditation self-help tapes designed to help us meet our past selves. They all support us to give ourselves permission to remember.

Distant memories are taking a more everyday place in the lives of people on a spiritual path, who are finding their far past as available to them as their night dreams, some of which may depict past-life stories. Particularly since the early 1980s, past lifetime memory has been valued in the field of personal growth. International teachers and popular seminars encouraging personal investigation have enabled people to demonstrate that far memory is a natural function, as safe as dreaming.

Exploring through self-help tapes is a useful beginning. But it is not past lifetimes counselling, unless you know how to use the life story material to make a difference now. Reaching an 'Aha!' point is valuable. 'Now I know why I'm so afraid of water' is helpful. But the question is — now that you know why, what are you doing about it? To accomplish change, inner work needs to be undertaken with one or more past selves, to lessen or eliminate the phobia. Sometimes one session with a professional is enough, providing the individual is doing the experiencing, rather than being told of a past life.

Today, so many people who utilise personal growth techniques are discovering the exciting ability to stop feeling like victims of life. They are learning to bring to conscious awareness the real causes of their own present unsatisfactory life situations. This is the new metaphysics: *meta* meaning beyond, *physics* the material. In the holistic sense metaphysics means ultimate causation — the individual factor in consciousness that sets material conditions in motion.

And as an avenue of metaphysical self-healing, past-life work often goes beyond therapy, into transcendental realms that require both participant and guide to move through sometimes unusual and bizarre experiences, and some that can be temporarily frightening.

Being frightened does not necessarily mean we are in danger. Facing and moving through fears is a basic necessity of personal growth, if we wish to develop.

DIFFERING STATES OF CONSCIOUSNESS

Many people feel that they've got enough to cope with in this life, without worrying about any other! Although they may be right, that logic misses the point.

In the here and now of daily living, the here is not always now, the now is not always here. We constantly and naturally dart into different states of consciousness, perhaps without realising it, looking for insight, memories, answers, comfort, new ideas, analysing the past or speculating about the future.

We have strange experiences in the twilight zone of going into or out of sleep, in dreams, during sex, under anaesthetic and in other drug-induced states, in illness, at near-death and death.

Obviously, it is impossible to live fully in the present moment while we are carrying invisible burdens from the past, because in various ways our attention is drawn back to unfinished business. Present problems often echo past problems. Old challenges keep repeating in the present. Have you ever asked, 'Why do I always act this way, when I don't want to?'

The past unfinished business of our present self lives on in our blocks and limitations, in recurring behaviour and situations that puzzle and stress us, even sometimes in bodily conditions. Chances are, we have been dealing with similar issues in other lifetimes.

A woman asking 'Why do I attract men with alcohol problems?' finds that in a previous lifetime she was herself an alcoholic member of an Irish alcoholic family, in an oppressed society where alcohol was used as a panacea. In addition to working through influences in her present-life childhood, she now has a further way to deal with underlying causes of the present pattern of suffering.

As I see it, by reliving this Irish story, by understanding and even by making new choices within it, she is likely to be healing deep origins of the attraction within herself. She is simultaneously releasing pressures from the present, and reducing the power of her unconscious compulsion to attract such problems to her.

Just as significant traces remain in you of the child and the adolescent you once were — not always to your present advantage— so traces of significant past selves may be felt, recognised, and released if they do not serve you now. Or, if they are healthily supportive, you may consciously integrate them for unsuspected benefits.

In everyday life, we are continually checking back into learned behaviour. In reincarnation therapy, there is even a theory that at times of important choice, the present self calls for a lightning-quick meeting with a relevant past self, receives advice, returns to the present, then wipes the meeting from conscious awareness. If this is true, how important that we heal and re-educate such inner advisors! If a past self's answer to opposition was to get drunk, or to kill, we could be in trouble!

HOPE FOR THE MENTALLY DISTURBED?

Tools of integration now available to psychiatrists through past lifetimes therapy may even offer hope to some of the mentally disturbed people who lose their own boundaries and believe they are Jesus, Napoleon, the Devil, Joan or Arc and other famous figures. (Contrary to general myth, comparatively few clients of past lifetimes therapists regress to lives of famous people.)

Experimental findings are that, in particular cases, some behaviour labelled psychotic is in fact accelerated spiritual emergence which has become spiritual emergency. Guidelines are now available to indicate where this could be happening, (see the book*The Stormy Search for the Self* by Christina Grof and Dr Stanislav Grof). When treated appropriately — usually by non-drug methods — individuals in such states have moved through confused and painful phases to a higher state of sanity, according to health professionals working in these new areas.In 1980 Christina Grof founded the international Spiritual Emergence network, a referral and education service for people in transformational crisis. The address of S.E.N.in Australia appears at the end of this book.

While research is still tentative, another theory emerging is that some mental illness may be the result of an individual becoming unconsciously stuck in confused life stories, where two or more past lifetimes have become superimposed on the present life. In the 21st century, professional untangling and resolving of these experiences could offer a way out to some. New metaphysical therapies are already beginning to attract in-depth research and development.

In the meantime, a commonsense caution to amateur regressionists: do not attempt past lifetime regression with anyone who is mentally disturbed, or with people under the influence of drugs, including alcohol.

WIDER HORIZONS

Whatever your views on reincarnation, this book may lead you past your comfort zone. The accounts reported here open wider horizons than you may yet feel comfortable with. For example, one concept that can disturb us is that we may have existed as life forms other than human.

Because life stories have a resonance all their own, reading this book may trigger your own emotions. You may find that you react with excitement, hostility, wonder, laughter, apprehension, grief, disapproval, joy, disbelief, even spiritual illumination. Traces of your own unrecognised memories may stir in deep places, as you encounter those of others.

I suggest you notice all your emotional reactions and treasure each one. You are going deeper within yourself by even considering the information. Be aware of what is happening in your body. Hear what you think to yourself. Catch and note any fleeting impressions of other people, events, places. Get familiar with how your own doubts and negative judgments tend to squash delicate impressions and stop their flow.

This is all practice for regression. To evaluate any experience, you must first have the experience. Allow it, and later evaluate it. By the end of the book you may have let yourself contact more of your own soul history.

BUT IS IT TRUE?

Whenever Westerners have looked on past-life memories as more than a curiosity, they have mostly examined them either to prove or to disprove them historically. Sometimes my clients are intrigued enough to compare their memories with historians' views of the past, or they rush off to check maps or encyclopedias. Sometimes their memories' accuracies amaze them. But usually time travellers are content with the importance of the experience to their lives now.

A few of the following accounts are from my own explorations. I am both believer and agnostic. What I have found true is that I can trust the process of transformation. When past-life work is conducted with integrity, however incomprehensible the imagery may be, I see that the psyche is following its own high purposes. In my experience,with inner exploration, when we ask with strong intention, we receive.

For clarity and convenience, from now on I will refer to past lifetimes impressions as though they are our true, lost memories. Perhaps they are.

In some quarters, reincarnational history is now considered a possible factor in the formation of both character and physical bodies, of behavioural patterns, and of mental, emotional and spiritual health. After my years of learning from the practice of past lifetimes counselling, I see that it opens up important issues around primal health, prenatal psychology,

17

psychic abilities, life-long imprints of birth, possibilities of death imprints, supposed connection with other dimensions and orders of being — that is, personal and universal metaphysics.

This whole extensive arena comprises one of the new frontiers of consciousness. Yet it is accessible, relatively simply, to the explorers among us: a birthright that is being newly discovered.

Chapter Two

Reincarnation : true or false?

An Indian girl aged about ten, Reena Gupta, told her family that before her birth she had been a woman murdered by her husband — who was still alive. She gave his name and address.

Reena's family took her to the address. The man was just out of gaol, having served ten years for murdering his wife.

Reena was fearful of him, but overjoyed to meet his children. She felt she had given them birth, out of a previous body.

(paraphrased from *The Case for Reincarnation* by Joe Fisher)

No matter how many millions of Easterners have accepted reincarnation as a fact of life, Westerners are still most intrigued by personal experiences that seem to prove the theory. Numerous people have told me of their spontaneous past-life memories surfacing, for example, when they visited new places.

An Australian woman tourist found the walled city of Dubrovnic surprisingly 'special and familiar'. Later she discovered a past lifetime there. In 1991, when she heard a radio report that bombs were falling on Dubrovnic, she impulsively cried out, 'Leave my city alone !'

While I was enjoying a visit to a beautiful nineteenth-century National Trust house in Tasmania I came to a roped-off nursery full of period toys. and I into tears, mystifying myself. Later I connected with the life of an English widow who had lived in a similar house. Her young son had gone to sea and never returned.

Years after a man's first visit to Scotland, he was still shaking his head in wonder. Driving as a tourist, he began to recognise countryside he had not seen before. He told his wife that a particular castle, their destination, would be around the next bend. It was. He took her to an upper room, having first described it correctly. He recounted stories about the history of the castle, and later found some of them in the castle guidebook.

He could not explain this. He believed he had read nothing about the place beforehand. He could not remember this happening before or since. He pondered the likelihood of unknown ancestral memory, of some mysterious connection hidden in his genes.

Another man driving in the British Isles had a similar experience. But he believed he understood it well. He also believed he had physical evidence proving the truth of his recall. This was the English psychiatrist, Dr Arthur Guirdham, who wrote several books about spontaneous recall of other lives, occurring over several years, for a number of people who felt they had incarnated as a group at particular times in history. At the time of recall, these people lived in England and other countries.

As a self-confessed sceptic, Dr. Guirdham began observing the experiences reported by this group. His initial role was to painstakingly check with historical records 'facts' from other times emerging unbidden from people's memories. He could not explain why these were accurate in both broad picture and detail. Eventually, Dr Guirdham found powerful memories of his own surfacing spontaneously. He felt he contacted three lifetimes involved with other members of this group.

In one of his books, Dr Guirdham recorded that, in Surrey in 1973, he drove his car past an alley formed of brick walls. He clearly recalled building the walls himself, in a past life, 170 years before. He felt that at the time he was a French stonemason, taken prisoner by the British during the Napoleonic wars, quartered in a fort in that district, and employed by neighbouring landholders. Inside the fort, he found symbols gouged in stone, corresponding with images he had seen first in the mind of that French stonemason.

In 1976, this psychiatrist — who spurned regression techniques — wrote that what he had lived through in those three lifetimes explained his present character to him more clearly than did current psychiatric theory.

One of the many more accounts of group reincarnation comes from California. Under hypnosis by Dr Marge Rieder, more than 15 people have recalled extensive detail of other lives and joint events in the same obscure town in rural Virginia, Millboro, during the American Civil War. None had been to Millboro in their present lifetimes, until some of them visited and identified localities as they had been last century.

TAJ MAHAL STIRS MEMORY

As a tourist in India, American physician Gladys McGarey inadvertently confronted possibilities of her own reincarnation.

The daughter of medical missionaries working in India, she had been born in a Presbyterian hospital near Agra, the city of the Taj Mahal. Her mother had told her how, just before the birth, she had taken her other children to view the magnificent building, created by the seventeenth-century Mogul emperor, Shah Jahan, as a memorial for his beautiful wife. As soon as Gladys's mother looked at the memorial she felt her first labour pain.

Soon after Gladys's birth in the hospital, a noise startled her mother, who jumped out of bed and began haemorrhaging. She lost so much blood that she was unable to breastfeed the baby.

On Gladys's return visit to India from the United States, she and her doctor husband, Bill, took a tour bus headed for the Taj Mahal. The driver told the story of the death of the emperor's wife, who had accompanied him into war even though pregnant with her fourteenth child. The baby was delivered in a tent near the battlefield, but the mother haemorrhaged, the midwife was unable to stop the bleeding, and the empress died.

Gladys recalled in an article for *Healing Currents*, the international journal of the Whole Health Institute, 'Listening to this story, I felt as though a hot poker had been stuck up my back. I was startled by my own reaction, never having felt anything like that before.' At her first sight of the Taj Mahal, Gladys began to cry, and continued to cry throughout the tour. Back at her hotel she fell into a deep sleep. Awakening, she said to herself, 'Why do you feel so badly? You helped her through 13. She died with the fourteenth.'

Gladys says, 'Suddenly I realised that I had been the midwife. My grief was rooted in events over three centuries old.' (Had the emperor ordered his usual punishment of beheading for the midwife, or torture with a hot poker? And had Gladys's mother perhaps been the empress — or her baby?)

Looking at the connections with her own birth of haemorrhage, midwifery and the Taj Mahal, Gladys also questioned coincidence in her choice of a profession that required her to spend much of her present lifetime coping with complicated births.

Back in the United States, Gladys and Bill began to investigate the medical case records of the American 'sleeping prophet', Edgar Cayce, which included reincarnational concepts. In 1970, they founded a Cayce-inspired medical centre for holistic healing in Phoenix, Arizona. Gladys believed that whole person healing concepts, including the spiritual dimension, had given her a deeper understanding of the Christian faith. She declared that this 'helped me to become a better physician, by sharing responsibility for healing with my patients rather than taking it from them'.

CHILDREN'S MEMORIES
Some of the most impressive documentation of apparent reincarnation comes from studies of children, who are less likely than adults to be influenced into past lifetime memories by education, religious concepts or other people's accounts.

In 1977, the prestigious *American Journal of Nervous and Mental Disease* acclaimed a world study by Dr Ian Stevenson, a professor of psychiatry at the University of Virginia Medical School. The journal announced Dr Stevenson's publication of five large volumes of case histories of children around the world who provided often detailed evidence of previous lives, usually 90 per cent accurate.

Dr Stevenson continues to publish volumes and by 1994 had documented nearly 2600 such cases. He does not use hypnosis. He has found that children's memories often include instances of violent death. He examined more than 200 birthmarks on children who claimed to have been killed by bullets or bladed weapons that injured those parts of the body in previous lives. He has found some corroborating evidence from medical records on the relevant deceased.

A three-year-old American child proved her case, a reincarnation investigator, Hemendra Banerjee, reports. Romy Crees, aged three, of Des Moines, Iowa, continually prattled of a previous life as a man in a nearby town. She gave names, told of his family's illnesses and events, and details of his death after a motorcycle accident.

Romy yearned to visit this former self's mother. Eventually, on the child's directions her family located the mother, then 76 years old. They took Romy to see her. The woman protested, 'I don't know you or anyone else in Des Moines!' Romy astonished her by relating intimate family history and identifying family members in photographs.

HIDDEN STRESS ON CHILDREN

Researcher Joe Fisher has pointed out that thousands of young children around the world say things like 'when I was big', complain about their small bodies restricting them, about being a different sex, about missing former people they loved, missing former food, clothes, lifestyle, even alcohol, tobacco or drugs. Some exhibit phobias relevant to their stories of violent death, such as of water, cars, knives.

Fisher makes the point that many children in this situation are not helped to neutralise their fears, frustrations, grief and confusion, because they are seldom believed. I add that these emotions do not go away but are largely repressed, providing a ground for later unhappiness.

The twentieth-century Indian teacher who introduced yoga to America and the Western world in 1920, Paramahansa Yogananda, spoke about his misery as a young Bengali child who recalled previous incarnations. In particular, he remembered a life as a yogi in the Himalayas. One result was that he found infancy humiliating and confusing. In his book *Autobiography of a Yogi* he stated that before he could speak, his thoughts came in many languages. But he could only express his distress in bouts of frustrated crying which his family could not understand. He added that many yogis are born with such knowledge.

DISTINGUISHED PIONEERS

Edgar Cayce, the famous American psychic, could be classed as the father of past lifetimes therapy. Cayce (1877-1945) was a relatively uneducated man who, in deep trance, gave more than 30 000 detailed life and health readings. His case records are available for research. Among them are 2500 psychic readings involving reincarnational details that Cayce's trance personality claimed were currently influencing the lives of people asking for help. People sought help because of ill health, deformity, marital unhappiness, professional and commercial problems and for vocational guidance.

Cayce counselled them that to dream of one's past lifetimes

quickened an individual's spiritual core.

Modern pioneers of past lifetimes therapy and/or reincarnation research since its upsurge in the 'fifties include distinguished psychiatrists, psychologists, physicians, hypnotherapists and lay people in various countries. Their own findings convinced some practitioners of the reality of reincarnation, while others remained questioning. All agreed that for regression subjects, the experiences were psychologically real.

In the 'fifties, American psychologist Dr Gina Cerminara began to annotate Edgar Cayce's views on the influence of past lives on present lives, claiming in her books that this presented a new dimension in psychology. In the same decade, in Cornwall, England, English hypnotherapist Arnall Bloxham regressed 50 people to 400 lives. A BBC television program investigated some of these in relation to their verifiable historical material.

In the 'fifties too, inspired by English psychiatrist Alexander Cannon's past lifetime regression of 1400 volunteers, an American businessman and amateur hypnotist, Morey Bernstein, regressed housewife Virginia Tighe to a life as an Irishwoman of earlier times. When he published *The Search for Bridey Murphy,* the book aroused intensive investigation of its regression detail, much of which checked out historically. But this credibility was undermined when people discovered Virginia had lived as a child with a Scottish-Irish aunt, who had often talked to her about Ireland.

Despite discrepancies between the aunt's knowledge and Bridey's knowledge, most people took this as proof that the recall was not genuine past-life memory. But Bernstein had initiated a new level of interest in past lifetimes regression and therapy.

In 1964, in California, Dr Morris Netherton reported being healed of stomach ulcers after he regressed to feeling he was someone else: a Mexican landowner kicked in the solar plexus by prison guards. A probation officer at the time, Netherton began to develop his regression techniques with teenagers in his care — with remarkable results, including the disappearance of physical ailments. He founded a lineage of regression therapy that does not use hypnosis.

In the 'sixties, psychologist Dr Helen Wambach was at first upset by a spontaneous past lifetime memory which challenged her conventionality. As a tourist visiting a small Quaker library, she was drawn inexorably to a particular book. She felt that, as another person, she had often read this book while riding a mule, and she knew its contents before she turned pages.

For ten years, Dr Wambach asked herself if this was fantasy, or an unsuspected reality? After conducting a replication study involving more than 2000 hypnotic regressions to past lives, she found her answer in numerical form. Her subjects classified into 49.4 per cent past lives as women and 50.6 per cent past lives as men — the percentage accepted as biological fact in relevant time periods.

Around the same time, after psychologist Dr Edith Fiore discovered through hypnosis that some of her patients' problems originated in the birth canal or the womb, she guided a patient to follow through on a memory of another lifetime, although she believed it was fantasy. Next time she saw him, he said he was free of sexual problems. She then explored many other patients' past lifetime memories, although she did not claim that their 'incredible' therapeutic results proved reincarnation.

In the 'seventies, the eminent American consciousness researcher and psychiatrist, Dr Stanislav Grof, developed an experiential self-discovery technique, featuring intense breathing as a replacement for LSD therapy. As well as stimulating the reliving of birth episodes, this 'holotropic therapy' technique triggers spontaneous experiences Dr Grof believes can be interpreted as memories of previous incarnations.

Such memories are activated through this technique within a range of other spontaneous spiritual, or transpersonal, and perinatal phenomena which he has categorised as a new model of the human mind. Dr Grof describes this realm of self-discovery as being of such significant therapeutic value that it suggests an entirely new orientation in psychiatric therapy. He has documented his findings in a number of books.

Since the 'seventies, American hypnotherapist/author Dick Sutphen has taken thousands of people to past lifetimes through hypnosis in private and group sessions. He has specialised in investigating man/woman relationships through their reincarnational histories.

In the 'eighties, Canadian psychiatrist Dr Joel Whitton

wrote in his book *Life Between Life* of witnessing a patient's unintentional foray into a between-lives state. He then spent years investigating patients' accounts of both past lifetimes and this state, including how they chose their parents before birth. He believes that the concept of continuing rebirth fosters responsibility in this life.

Australia's Dr Peter Ramster worked with some clients who regressed to past lives in Europe. He took these people to the locales of their stories in Europe. On television, most recognised places unseen in their present lifetimes but described in their regressions. One woman discovered a tiled floor she had visualised in regression, by digging through a deep layer of soil covering a henhouse floor.

New York Jungian psychotherapist Dr Roger Woolger tells his clients to follow any story that emerges through their exploration of problems, as if it were a real-life story. He encourages them to relive as that other self, through trauma release to completion, whether or not they believe in reincarnation.

The world listing of past lifetimes therapists grows as useful results accumulate and similar findings emerge, often from practitioners working independently.

In *Vibrational Medicine*, a 1988 survey of newly recognised alternative healthcare modalities that involve the body's subtle energies, American physician Dr Richard Gerber includes past lifetimes therapy with others he reports are shaping up to form a major healthcare category in the 21st century.

CHRISTIAN ATTITUDES TO REINCARNATION
Many people fascinated by the dance of incarnation regard themselves as Christians although reincarnation is not a part of orthodox Christian teachings.

Bible scholars tell us that references to reincarnation were censored from the Bible after a group of Christian bishops vetoed it through a series of councils in Constantinople, beginning in AD 325. Justinian 1, Emperor of the Eastern Roman Empire, denounced 'the monstrous restoration of rebirth' in AD 553. (Reincarnation was referred to as the doctrine of rebirth.) The Church's literal rejection was of all references pertaining to 'the pre-existence of the soul', thus denying previous lives. The bishops were proclaiming that eternity began at birth.

However, reincarnation buffs believe that, in spite of censoring, they can find a few remaining references in the Bible to what, historically, was a major interpretation of the meaning of life in the East in New Testament times.

One Biblical reference is in the seventeenth chapter of the *Gospel of St Matthew*. In the King James version, Jesus Christ answers his disciples' questions about Old Testament prophecy with, 'Elias truly shall first come, and restore all things. But I say unto you, that Elias is come already, and they knew him not, but have done unto him whatsoever they listed.' Then the disciples understood he meant that Elias 'was' John the Baptist, who had been beheaded by King Herod.

Researchers Sylvia Cranston and Carey Williams report in their book, *Reincarnation: A New Horizon in Science, Religion and Society* that, after AD 553, to believe in pre-existence of the soul brought ex-communication from the Christian Church.

Although Christian scholars today claim that a Church decree banning reincarnation was not officially passed, the spirit of massive disapproval of reincarnation thundered through official pronouncements for many centuries. Modern Christian anti-reincarnation sentiments have been undeniable. Many, if not most, victims of the mediaeval Church's wars and regimes of terror held spiritual attitudes that included reincarnational beliefs. Many believed in natural healing methods. Both outlooks encouraged people in self-responsibility rather than in reliance on priests to mediate between themselves and God.

One such group were the Cathar heretics. Catharism was a popular religion originating in Mediterranean countries around the eleventh century A.D. As most Cathar books were burned by the Inquisition, information on their doctrines is not extensive although Gnostic and Sufi influences are clear. Cathars believed in reincarnation, and placed a high value on introspection (discouraged by the Church), touch healing or 'the laying on of hands', God as love, and gender equality. Cathars honored women (often married) in their priesthood. The religion was eliminated through widespread murder, especially by burning, imprisonment, torture and terrorism executed by Christians over the twelfth and thirteenth centuries.

Such events have often come to life in my consulting room. People reliving those dramatic times recognise not only continuing influences in their present lives from such former atti-

27

tudes and events, but also feel that they recognise other people around them now as former companions, lovers, teachers, even persecutors.

For centuries, successive Popes waged wars against people who held beliefs differing from the Christianity of the time, and so did not support the power and wealth of the Church. Reincarnationists were among those burned at the stake. In the witch-hunt centuries, especially the sixteenth and seventeenth, natural healers and midwives in particular were persecuted and martyred. Modern perspective shows that both heretics and 'witches' tended to uphold values that did not support exploitation of either people or the natural world. One source claims that possibly nine million people were incinerated during the centuries of this mainly female holocaust.

Numbers of my clients have relived such scenes in the process of discharging hidden trauma that has been limiting them in the present. For them, reincarnation feels unpleasantly real, yet they say the recall enriches them both personally and spiritually.

Nowadays, a handful of Christian ministers write books seriously considering reincarnation. An example is the American Anglican priest/academic, Professor Geddes MacGregor, who classes reincarnation as one of the Christian tradition's 'hidden riches', on the basis of early records.

Even some Christian observers question whether the idea of reincarnation is more fantastic than the idea of resurrection of the flesh. Both Catholic and Protestant churches teach that when this world ends, the bodies of all who have died since Adam will be resurrected. Fundamentalist Christians teach that the fleshly bodies of the saved will be transformed and glorified, while the bodies of sinners will burn forever.

Now, after more than 1500 years of Christian prejudice against reincarnation, an irony for past-life counsellors and their clients is that many people regress to lifetimes as Christian nuns, monks and Church dignitaries.

Spiritual awareness has traditionally blended with healing. Throughout this book, by 'spiritual' I do not necessarily mean religious, or related to organised belief. Nor do I mean simply the non-material. I mean the spiritual urge now esteemed by many as innate in human beings, even if undeveloped — the urge to unite with the greater or higher self within, to become all that we are capable of becoming, to personally contact the divine while in the flesh. Dr Jean Houston describes this inner journey in the title of her book on sacred psychology as *The Search for the Beloved*.

The segment of humanity becoming consciously focused on this spiritual quest is already vast internationally. Both community leaders and 'ordinary' people are expressing idealistic values and mystical leanings that were unacceptable in mainstream Christian-based society even 20 years ago. Numbers of influential social commentators see this spiritual quickening as crucial to the personal and racial evolution of consciousness. They claim that the ensuing cultural shift has the potential to reshape our global civilisation.

GNOSTIC DOCTRINE

Dr Carl Jung and others considered that core ideas of Christianity are rooted in the ancient doctrines of Gnosticism, in which reincarnation was central. The Church, however, deemed Gnosticism heretical and destroyed many of its treatises. Gnostic traditions come down from Zoroaster, and from the Orphic mysteries as communicated through mathematician/philosopher Pythagoras. Judaism and Islam show Gnostic traces.

Gnostics taught in secret schools that man is redeemed and informed of his origin, essence and destiny only through personal divine revelation, not through scripture. His unconscious self has fallen from the Godhead into an alien material world, and he must become conscious through his intuition.

Gnosticism remained the domain of scholars until 1945, when an Arab farmer on a camel entered a Coptic graveyard in a town on the Nile, searching for fertiliser. He discovered an old earthernware jar full of documents that later proved to be early Gnostic writings. When the farmer took them home, his mother used a few sheets to feed her fire.

The remainder were considered so historically significant that major academic organisations, including the American Smithsonian Institute, financed the project to bring these 52 papyrus texts to the public.

The Gnostic authors of these documents, which were written in Greek at the same time as the New Testament, saw themselves as Christians preserving secret teachings of Jesus, until other people became spiritually mature enough to read them.

They record that Jesus taught reincarnation to his disciples, showing them how major personal shortcomings reverberate in a later life. In one dialogue, Mary speaks with Jesus about rebirth, curiously referring to it as 'coming in at another circuit'.

The Jung Institute in Zurich bought one of the Gnostic documents, the *Gospel of Thomas*. In 1977, an English translation of all the documents spurred a vigorous revival of Gnostic studies in the West.

Gnostics taught that worlds too are reborn. This becomes less preposterous to Western thought in the light of the work of renowned British scientist Professor James Lovelock who first discovered ozone-layer damage from chemicals. While working with NASA in the 'sixties, he began proposing that Earth was a self-regulating entity that keeps its climate and chemistry constant over time. He named the four-and-a-half-billion-year-old Earth Gaia, after a goddess of the ancient Greeks, some of whose philosophers taught reincarnation. The possibility that Earth is not an object but a being sparks visions of advanced versions of Gaia appearing over unimaginable timespans!

DIFFERING REINCARNATIONAL BELIEFS

Reincarnation is one of the oldest and most widely respected of human beliefs. For millennia it has underscored Eastern nations and tribal cultures as a source of divine inspiration and life philosophy. One of the oldest languages, Sanskrit, has words to describe traces of previous lives appearing in a present life: *karma*, meaning action, *vasana,* a past life memory, *samskara*, a dispositional tendency, *klesa*, a repetitive negative thought/emotion pattern.

Reincarnational philosophy appeared in the royal cult of the ancient Egyptian pharoahs, the mystery cult of Orpheus in second-century Greece, and in Manicheanism, a thir -century Persian religion. It was most elaborately developed in Asia through Hinduism, Buddhism, Jainism, Sikhism, and Sufism (the mystical branch of Islam).

Reincarnation in surviving ancient tribal cultures is linked to veneration of ancestors. In the Yorulba and Edo African tribes, each boy child is named 'Father Has Returned' and each girl child 'Mother Has Returned'.

Australian Aboriginal people believe that the spirits of humans periodically reincarnate in human, animal, insect or plant forms, and even as stones, water, fire, wind, sun, moon and stars. The Aboriginal tribe considers that to establish the identity of each reborn ancestor is vital because of the social importance of totems.

Reincarnation also affects the structure of Zulu society. Zulus believe that each living spirit experiences animal life, from insects to elephants, graduating into human form in which rebirth involves ancestors.

Many belief systems hold that reincarnation is not confined within the human race. Some suggest that before each of us reached human status, we have even perhaps existed as elemental forces.

Reincarnation also features in more modern schools of thought, such as theosophy and transpersonal psychology.

More than a third of the current world population accepts reincarnation. Cultural attitudes to rebirth range widely from the pessimism of the Hindus, viewing it as failure to attain a more exalted state, to the optimism of some African tribes, seeing it as renewed opportunity to improve the world of the living. In sub-Saharan tribes, failure to be reborn is regarded as an evil. Different belief systems estimate that periods between death and rebirth vary from immediate, to decades, to 1600 years or more.

In 1981, a U.S. Gallup Poll reported that almost one-quarter of adult Americans believed in reincarnation — more than 35 million people. Since then media focus shows rapidly increasing interest in the Western world. As a sign of the times, for example, contemporary public interest for some years supported a past lifetimes column in a major Australian women's magazine. On television programs viewed by more than 15 million people, American presenter Oprah Winfrey investigated both past-life memories of children, and breath regression techniques, in 1995.

BUDDHIST BELIEFS ABOUT REINCARNATION
Reincarnation implies that we are not so much a person who

has a soul, as we are a soul that has a person — perhaps many persons, perhaps thousands. The Cambridge English Dictionary defines 'soul' in part as 'essence'. Christians see a soul as an individual essence, an enduring higher selfhood. But must we have a soul in order to reincarnate?

Three hundred million Buddhists don't believe so, yet they believe in reincarnation. A central principle of Buddhism is that only an illusory ego reincarnates, they say, a 'no-self', a component of an entire universe that perishes and is created afresh in each instant.

The 14th Dalai Lama, the Tibetan Buddhist leader Tenzin Gyatso, has stated that reincarnation is a major factor in 'the development of that wisdom and compassion ultimately leading to the attainment of the fully enlightened state of a Buddha'. He himself, and the line of previous Dalai Lamas, were appointed to high office through extensive investigation into their personal reincarnation, as expressions of one being. This being was destined to be spiritual leader of a country the size of Western Europe, throughout centuries.

Following the Chinese invasion of Tibet, the present Dalai Lama escaped into exile in 1959. In recent years, he has earned the Nobel Peace Prize by travelling throughout Western countries as a spokesman for peace and the Buddhist way, drawing ever-larger crowds obviously hungering for spiritual leadership.

This man's discovery as a reincarnated Dalai Lama followed tradition. Some years after the previous Dalai Lama died in 1933, signs observed by lamas in meditation signalled search groups to set out eastward to find his reincarnated self as a small boy. One group travelled as far as a Chinese province where Tibetans lived.

These lamas interviewed many small Tibetan boys, until a two-year-old seized former possessions of the dead leader and spontaneously identified other lamas known to that leader, even though they had changed clothes with servants. Moles on the child's body were seen as traces of two extra arms of the god Chenrezi.

Monks ceremonially carried the boy into Lhasa on a golden palanquin to begin his new life in 1938. At the age of 15 he received extra powers as head of state, becoming a modern priest/king.

Other lamas demonstrate knowledge of previous incarnation — even from other countries. At age eight a British child became entranced with Tibetan iconography he found in a library, and wrote away for more information. As Ngakpa Chogyam Rinpoche, he now teaches Buddhism to Westerners. During adult study in India, he discovered he was a reincarnation of a female Buddhist lama who had died in an avalanche.

A profound old Tibetan ritual fleshes out the reincarnation concept even further, at least for Buddhists. Before the Communist Chinese decimated Tibetan culture, the Tibetan woman holding the office of Abbess of Samding was required to visit a special room. This contained the mummified remains of her predecessors — her previous selves. Later she would have joined them in death.

EXPLANATIONS FOR PAST LIFETIME RECALL

There is no gilt-edged guarantee that we live more than one lifetime.

Nor is there any gilt-edged guarantee that we live only one lifetime.

Answers to life's deep mysteries must, I believe, involve our personal truth. This demands a search.

Even in the multitude of reported cases worldwide where past-life impressions have been historically verified, there is no guarantee that the past-life traveller was that previous person. The known is only that such a person was documented to exist, and that the seeker seemed to have tapped into that particular life. The seeker may or may not be a direct psychic descendant of that person.

THEORIES DENYING REINCARNATION

Various theories deny reincarnation as an explanation of other-life recall.

One is cryptomnesia, which is recall of forgotten learning that seems new. A case considered by many to be cryptomnesia was the controversial Bridey Murphy story experienced by Virginia Tighe. The assumption was that Virginia had consciously forgotten information from an old aunt, but unknowingly reported it through a fictional past self, although this claim has been challenged.

People who prefer to view past-life stories personally experienced as mind metaphors assume that a higher part of the mind presents these to illuminate aspects of the present life.

Another non-reincarnation theory cites temporary possession of a person by attaching spirits of former humans, believed to implant their own life memories for their own purposes.

More widespread is the belief that everything that has ever happened to any being at any level of consciousness is imprinted in the universal ether, an assumed all-pervading field of energy, or realm of consciousness. Occultists call this supposed bank of information the Akashic Records, and claim that it can be tapped. Someone apparently recalling past-life impressions would be subconsciously retrieving relevant other-life imprints from this central pool of consciousness. Jung's theory of a realm of a 'collective unconscious' is allied.

Also in line with this viewpoint is the radical morphic resonance hypothesis of British biologist Dr Rupert Sheldrake, published in 1981 as his *Theory of Formative Causation*. Now extensively tested, the morphic field resonance theory has become part of popular scientific mystique. Morphic means 'relating to life-form structure'. Physicists define 'fields' as interconnecting regions of physical influence that interrelate with matter, yet are not matter.

The theory suggests that we exist in an all-pervading energy field that derives its structure from the past. Our genes tune in to a morphic field for their make-up. Dr Sheldrake states that the global field of morphic resonance includes mental, behavioural, social, cultural and genetic fields. Our brains do not store memories, but act as receivers to draw out memories from a field. This would mean that we organise our behaviour through morphic fields.

These interrelating fields are not confined to our brains or bodies, but link to our environment. When such a field stops existing, through an individual's death, it disappears, but can appear again in other times and places complete with its information, or memory, of the previous existence.

This theory opens up new interpretations of memory, learning, health, heredity and evolution, all intimately related to reincarnation. Is it a scientific description of the field named the Akashic Records? Is this how the seeking human may unconsciously magnetise particular life stories helpful to his or her present state?

Or do we actually, personally, reincarnate? Or both?

ANCESTRAL MEMORY THEORY

Ancestral memory, or memory inherited directly through genes, is also a popular explanation for other-life recall. This implies that coded information, or memory, is contained in body cells transferred through sperm and ovum from one generation to the next. Past-life memories, then, would be memories from one's many physical ancestors.

Complications arise here when, say, a white-skinned person 'remembers' being a person of black, brown, yellow or red skin within recent times, when such a strain is not recently in the biological family.

Could the fabric of our being be intimately interwoven with both ancestors and previous selves? Certainly humans are complex enough to incorporate many influences.

Non-genetic biological memory transfer from one body/mind to another is also a real phenomenon, according to Dr William Byrne of Duke University, one of a number of biologists who have been testing it with worms and rodents. This research seems to demonstrate that while learning takes place in the brain, memory of what is learned may be stored throughout the body, and passed on non-sexually, even to other life forms, independently of the brain.

Bacteriologists are also investigating memory in a molecule (*New Scientist*, Sept.16, 1995). Bacteria — considered 'emotional' for having needs they act to satisfy — may pass information to others via chemicals.

WHY NOT IMAGINATION?

Some people attribute other-life recall to imagination. While this is a comfortable point of view for anyone threatened by the idea that past lifetime memories could be running loose in the population, experienced past-life practitioners — the specialists who actually observe large numbers of regressions — are not satisfied with this explanation. Do people imagine the accompanying extreme and sustained emotions? How do they retain cohesiveness when their guide jumps them about in time within stories they do not consciously know? Why do recallers not change stories as they go along, to edit out trauma? How can these stories produce present change, even at the physical level?

Psychologist Dr Edith Fiore concluded that either large numbers of people have reincarnated, or that they all have the most creative imaginations imaginable.

THE OCCULT IN THE LABORATORY

As we come to understand more about the living process that is the human race, we are discovering keys to mysteries formerly seen as occult (meaning hidden). Reincarnation may be one of these.

The supernatural is daily becoming more easily seen as the operation of natural laws, as scientists begin to unlock, for example, properties of crystals (magic wands), hidden sensitivities and chemical qualities of plants, fungal cultures and such items as skin of toad (witch's brews, shamanic healers' potions, folk remedies) and mysterious methods of communication from mind to mind (telepathy). During the last 20 years, U.S., Russian and Japanese governments have spent millions of dollars researching remote viewing, or extra-sensory perception, abilities, for application to military purposes.

Even abilities of the human organism to move matter without physical touch or force are being recognised, as Western parapsychologists stop wondering if psychokinesis exists and emulate Russian scientists in studying its effects. A Princeton University team of physicist and psychotherapist, investigating manipulation of matter by non-visible human means, prosaically labelled their research 'Engineering Anomalies'. Their results in psychokinesis and remote viewing investigation appear in their book, *Margins of Reality*.

In the 'seventies, Israeli psychic/showman Uri Geller was spectacularly successful in introducing spoon-bending to the world public. After his radio and television demonstrations triggered metal objects to bend mysteriously in thousands of homes in many countries where people listened to or watched him, many well-known scientists investigated him, looking for the unknown natural force. While this is still largely a mystery, people now bend spoons at parties all around the U.S., taught by aerospace engineer Jack Houck and others.

If investigation should ever absolutely prove reincarnation, then some of our memories are centuries, even millennia, older than we are. This would mean that lifetimes of information have travelled with us between incarnations, when presumably we had no brains or bodies in which to store them.

How?

In this respect, each inner explorer is a researcher. Your personal laboratory is yourself. Everyone has the ability to contribute new knowledge of the deeper mysteries of being.

ARE ENERGY FIELDS THE KEY?

A long-time investigator of the human energy field, Professor William Tiller of the Department of Material Science and Engineering at Stanford University, California, has a theory about how we store past lifetime memories. Professor Tiller validates ancient mystical traditions that view the human being as a composite of interpenetrating energy fields, or bodies, each vibrating at a different frequency. The most dense, the physical body, is at their centre. Extending to close outside it is the body-shaped etheric field. Extending to outside that are the more oval, striated fields, or bodies, called the astral or emotional body, the mental body, and the causal body or Higher Self.

Professor Tiller agrees with Eastern tradition that these fields of subtle energy — biofields — traditionally called the aura, are the primary life force: the body does not create the fields. Biofields form a template, he says, from which the physical body is first and continuously created. He views the physical body as a teaching tool, a simulator, through which the activities and conditions of the subtle energy fields are expressed.

Following the invention of Kirlian electrophotography in Russia in the 1960s, which some believe photographs the etheric field of life forms, new scientific instruments are being refined to detect more of these biofields, and to utilise them to diagnose disease before it manifests at the physical level.

Supporting Professor Tiller's work are findings from another of the new breed of scientists pioneering in this vibrational field — beyond the limits of the Newtonian, or purely mechanistic, scientific view of the universe. Twenty years ago, Professor Valerie Hunt, of University of California Los Angeles, while using conventional equipment for measuring electric potential of human muscles, detected previously unrecorded electrical oscillations radiating from the body. She believed this activity was unknown to science. She confirmed this as the human energy field, or aura.

37

Professor Hunt went on to make electromyograms (EMGs) of the frequencies and behaviour of subtle energies operating most strongly around the sites of what Eastern religions call 'chakras', or 'lotuses of light'. These are vortices within the biofield which loosely correspond to the position of the body's glands. Her instruments confirmed vibrations of color as seen within this field by sensitives. She proved that the aura responds to stimuli even before the brain does. Human energy field data from an electrode gave her, she believes, the first true chaos pattern discovered within a major electro-biological system. Now Professor Hunt believes that the human energy field contains, as well as electromagnetic energy, an unidentifed energy.

PAST LIFETIME MEMORIES STORED?
Professor Tiller postulates that when we die, we drop off, along with the body, the close layers of the biofield, and we continue existence after death as an energy unit composed of the three outer fields (the soul?). *These three levels of energy, he suggests, are where our multiple lifetime memories are encoded.*

Each subtle body, or layer of the human energy field, he claims, is a tuned circuit that enables a human being to tap energy from the cosmos, or to contact other aspects of his or her being. (This is a reminder of the Gnostic writings, where Mary says to Jesus that reincarnating is 'coming in at another circuit'.)

In this view, past lifetimes therapy activates the outer layers of a person's biofield, or aura, which resonate through the present mind, emotions and body, thus uniting past and present experiences.

Dr Deepak Chopra, international author and lecturer on medicine and spirituality, describes the human body as a field of ideas.

Physician Dr Richard Gerber states that field-of-energy medicine sees the physical body as a suit of clothing made of chemicals, which we as spiritual beings put on to experience life in physical form. Perhaps ancient Arabs agreed. Their word for reincarnation is *taqamus*, which literally means 'changing one's shirt'.

ELASTIC NOTIONS OF TIME
Now that popular thought is beginning to embrace essential

concepts of quantum or subatomic science, many of us are grappling with vast possibilities. We are told that our familiar material world is made up of vibrating particles that can turn into waves; some are invisible, some are only probable, some seem to travel backwards in time. Among such apparent impossibilities, living one life after another may not seem so outlandish — until we come to the new physicists' claim that linear time is an illusion, that actually all time is simultaneous.

This is not totally new. Pioneer consciousness explorer Dr Sigmund Freud taught that in the human unconscious there is no time. Einstein said, 'The distinction between past, present and future is only an illusion.' Now a former protege of Einstein's, leading theoretical physicist Dr David Bohm, adds his view that physically, through a newly perceived enfolding and unfolding nature of reality, the past actively exists in the present.

To attempt to grasp these bewildering ideas we might turn to the hologram, a three-dimensional picture created by laser beam. Every small part of a holographic film contains the image of the whole. Some scientists now see the cosmos as a giant hologram, the human brain as a hologram, human memory as a hologram, also the human body. Human beings are seen as a frequency phenomenon, self-converting into holographic forms. Everyday 'reality' itself could be a holographic image, a kind of created illusion with multiple depths.

One of the countless implications of these controversial assertions is, that if the brain is a hologram — if we view an individual's range of consciousness as a hologram — a part (a present lifetime) would contain the whole (past or future lifetimes), accessible under appropriate conditions.

Often people's everyday words seem to hint at such a holographic nature, when we listen carefully. A man describes an emotional shock: 'When I was nineteen, I had the legs cut from under me.' Another describes a recurring back pain: 'It feels like a knife going into me.' A woman says, 'When I get depressed it feels like I'm going under for the last time with nobody to help.'

A woman recalled that in a past lifetime she had a son who, at the age of ten, died from illness. She described her shock and grief then as, 'I feel I'm being ripped apart.' That son, she feels, was the same entity who is now her teenage son. In this life, he was born by Caesarean section, which literally ripped her apart.

POWER IN THE PRESENT MOMENT

In 1790 Goethe wrote, 'The present moment is a powerful goddess.' Today's personal growth disciplines emphasise that the present is the point of power. There could be far more to the present moment than we thought.

In the present moment we can travel within consciousness and simultaneously heal old hurts and misconceptions in our other lives. As we now joyfully embrace memories of former happiness, rich personal qualities and capabilities, we are both healing and reclaiming present hidden aspects of our own deep psyche.

In that context — however exciting the various theories of reality are — as a self-transformation consultant, I consider it irrelevant whether time is linear or simultaneous, or whether reincarnation can or cannot be proven historically true. I tell people who want me to make up their minds for them about reincarnation: 'You yourself have that precious privilege.'

NOW THE LOTUS....

A poem written by a past self, an ancient priest

The lotus is a symbol for infinity.
It floats upon the waters of the unconscious,
where time is not.

The roots of the lotus reach deep into primeval mud
    from which life springs.
Beauty from formlessness : this is the human creation.

The power of the lotus is in its perfection of the moment
    with no beginning
    and no end
    and many parts at once.

Work with perfection NOW.

There is indeed a future state of perfection —
    but it is another lotus.

The lotus swims in its pool.
It is a symbol.
Do not be limited by your symbols.

PART TWO:

HOW HAS PAST LIFETIMES COUNSELLING HELPED?

Chapter Three

Lovers

A South American girl tearfully farewells her family, and enters a large flat-topped pyramid, a stone temple. She has been dedicated for life as a priestess, and must be free from the distractions of normal living.

She is expected to open her psyche to cosmic gods, in service to the jungle community whose dwellings surround the pyramid. Her mentor is a priest, a severe man who also lives in the temple.

Throughout decades she ceremonially inhales herbal aromas that induce trancelike states, to relay prophecy from the gods. The pair hold ceremonies on top of the temple, with the people below arrayed in brilliant feather costumes.

The child grows into a woman who loves her vocation — and who also loves the priest, as he has grown to love her. But their vows prevent them from making love, for the whole of their lives.

When freedom eventually arrives for these two, it is in England in the 1980s. Former priestess and priest are both schoolteachers. She is unhappily married. When they first meet she again thinks he is remote. Later, when their new love story unfolds, and he again guides her on an emerging spiritual path, they become lovers. Now they have been married for eleven years and have two children.

'After the birth of our first child,' she recalls, 'I found love-making particularly painful. I discovered that I was punishing myself for having broken that ancient taboo. Then I allowed myself to feel forgiveness, knowing that the integrity my husband and I share for each other isn't ruled by taboo, but by allowing.'

Her husband has not explored his reincarnational background, but he has a dim awareness of canoeing fearfully into a dark cave with a woman, towards a ritual death.

SOUL-DEEP QUEST
Reunion for lovers encompasses fires of the heart leaping

centuries — twin torches lighting trails from country to country, blazing through from one culture, one hemisphere, into another. The soul-deep quest is to find someone who will understand something that cannot be explained, who will love beyond reason.

The awesome powers of love can motivate many lifetimes. The drives that lovers share give rise to the concept of soulmates, those who have merged deep loving feelings in other lifetimes. Many pray to find a soulmate now, while some believe they have found that soulmate, even more than one.

How is it that individuals who feel they have been lovers in one lifetime can find each other in another lifetime, perhaps crossing today's world to do it? Unknowingly seeking each other among the almost six billion people on the planet today, they not only meet but fuse into emotional partnership.

Some couples believe they have shared more than two lifetimes — four, maybe eight, or more — although perhaps not all in the roles of lovers. Are their meetings coincidental? What are the odds, among the 50 billion people who have ever been on the planet? Not coincidence, no. Some deep law of attraction is at work here, transcending boundaries of time and space.

Mysteries of close relating can defy logic. A woman of 60 claims that her present husband of a 20-year marriage appeared to her in phantom form when they were children. She says, 'I was about six, at the beach on an island off England with my parents. I saw a boy a bit older than me walking by the water. For some reason I ran to talk to him. Afterwards he faded away. It was my present partner.' Her partner was at the time unknown and on the other side of the world, has never been to that island, and is sceptical of psychic events.

Love at first sight, that whole-being shock, recognition beyond words of deep bonds with someone new.... It happened to a man who had awakened to profound depths in himself, through sessions of rebirthing *(see Appendix)*. He said, 'I'm in love! I've only just met her. I've known her before. I want to know what happened then.'

Cliches are often repeated truth. People do say from their hearts, 'As soon as I met him I knew I'd known him forever', or 'The moment I saw him, I knew we'd be together forever'. And they are awed by the power of these feelings.

Sometimes lovers feel they are twin souls. These are apparent strangers who become so close that they may think and feel almost as one being, seemingly because of a bonding in many more lives than one. Trance channeller Edgar Cayce had a son called Hugh Lynn Cayce. Hugh Lynn's widow, Sally, said of her psychic closeness to her husband that she could just think of him and know his whereabouts, his thoughts and feelings.

'How do I love thee ?' asked poet Elizabeth Barrett Browning. 'Let me count the ways.' In past-life terms — possibly as a Greek peasant, a Chinese noblewoman, a Welsh coalminer, a Pacific Islander, a Saracen soldier, a French conman, an Indian beggar girl, a politician from North America, or more. Understanding the secrets of our relationships here and now can be a full-time job, let alone — we might think — exploring such multilevel intimacies. But rather than complicating the issues, past lifetimes recall offers doorways to richer relating.

Through examples, we see how love can bind people together over two or more lifetimes. It seems we continue to incarnate together when we have something special to enjoy, to learn, to give or to receive. More than two individuals may be involved, and sequential partners may also come to us from the past.

Stories of reunited lovers are not always happy-ever-after, because even soulmates are still learning. For example, John Lennon and Yoko Ono believed they had been lovers in another time, yet they separated this time even before he was murdered. Even twin souls may part — perhaps because, after, say, 20 shared journeys, one or both desire something new! But let's look at some heart-glow accounts of lovers rediscovering each other.

LOVE THEN AND NOW

A woman says of the father of her child, 'I feel irrevocably bound to him at soul level. I can't commit to another man'. She discovers a past life as a woman in Wales where she and the same individual were blissfully married until he died through accident. After regression her arm feels sore. I encourage her physically to reach out and imagine holding her past-life husband close. She does, and weeps. The pain leaves.

A girl confides, 'My current boyfriend and I feel we've known each other before'. She finds that they had spent six lives together as love partners, and that some unresolved emotional issues trailed them through time. Their most recent meeting occurred in England during World War II. After they married he served as a Royal Air Force pilot while she, a young mother, sheltered in tunnels during the London bombings. They lost each other abruptly when she died in a traffic accident. Drawn together again now by love, these two have resumed the joys and lessons of a primary relationship.

A current marriage of 39 years began apparently through a mistake, half a world away. Second cousins Greta and Hans had known and liked each other as children in Germany. After Hans emigrated to Australia Greta migrated too, to marry a friend of his. But soon after she arrived this relationship foundered. Hans was close by to comfort her. They are still together. Says Hans, 'We think and feel alike. We have a few differences, but we are so close. And two reputable clairvoyants have "seen" independently that we are twin souls.'

Hans spent his first regression with tears streaming down his face as the story he discovered tapped deep wells of joy and sadness. His first inner picture was of a man in his thirties in Russia, watching his beloved wife, Anna, die slowly of tuberculosis. The man was a doctor. Patients came from far and wide to consult him yet he could not save his wife's life. Hans immediately recognised the dying woman as a past self of his wife.

As Peter, Hans relives a happy family boyhood, gruelling years of study to achieve his ambition to become a doctor, and his meeting with the beautiful Anna whom he loves at first sight (a hint of even previous involvement). On the day Peter receives his doctorate scroll, the two are married in a big country church in the presence of their approving families. Both Peter and Anna are ecstatic at their good fortune. They set up house and medical practice together, he as a herbalist and she as a hands-on healer. After dealing all day with patients they relax by walking together through beautiful meadows. 'Talking, talking,' he reports. 'So much to say, about everything! It seems one lifetime is not enough to say it all.'

Soon Anna begins to tire easily. Her health deteriorates. Peter treats her with everything he knows and takes her to other healers, but she does not respond. Over five years she moves steadily towards death. 'I can't cure her,' her husband sobs. 'I love her so.'

Peter is with her when she dies. He wants to die too. Yet at the funeral many in the crowd attempt to comfort him, by talking about his work. He says, 'I know I can still help many people.'

At 50 Peter develops pain, self-diagnoses cancer and becomes bedridden. His mind is flooded with expectation that after death he will be reunited with his adored Anna. He resolves that 'we will never be parted again'.

In their current incarnations, after tuberculosis has ceased to be a major scourge, Hans and Greta work together again in the field of natural medicine. They are dedicated to discovering unrecognised information on body energy systems, seeking breakthroughs to heal chronic illnesses.

THREATS FROM THE PAST

Sometimes past love relationships can threaten present relationships, as the following stories show. These married people, in crisis, turned to the past for help.

A man with a beloved wife and three sons fell in love with a stranger. He wavered between euphoria and fear for his marriage. Suspecting a past lifetime involvement, he decided to find out what was really going on.

In the Dark Ages in Europe, he and this stranger had been lovers. The sweet flames of that entanglement had leapt 1400 years. He recalled details and joys of how it had been for them then. Coming out of regression, he was rather surprised that his hunch had paid off. Three years later when we met socially, he drew me aside and told me that after the exploratory session the problem had melted away. The feelings ignited between him and the other woman had stabilised, so that his deeper memories of the heart no longer threatened his marriage.

A married woman who found herself loving both her husband and another man could not decide for one or the other. Close to nervous collapse, she explored a number of past lives with both men. Because of working through these long-ago stories, she found her attraction to the new man lessening. Finally, she found a lifetime where she had loved him desperately but he had stayed remote. Now she said, 'This time I feel it's been alright for me to take a long time to make up my mind. He's had to wait for me, for a change!' She chose then to stay with her husband.

A WARTIME LOVE

Bettina, a young married radio operator, suddenly became too stressed to go to work. She was prescribed anti-depressants to mask terror, weeping and chest pains, but came to me because she felt 'there's something deep going on in me, I have to get to it'. Initially she did not mention feeling unsettled in her marriage.

We found a number of past lives in which she had died violently around her present age, and in which people close to her had died. We also uncovered anxiety, guilt and yearning over a former love affair in her present life.

Exploring a previous lifestory involving her ex-lover, Bettina finds that, earlier this century, as an English teenager, Elizabeth, she met and married a man called Cliff. Elizabeth says, 'I love him with all my heart. He buys me beautiful things. He's devoted. I'm contented. We're having a picnic on a hill, with our little boy.' She relives fragments of their happiness in that life, sometimes crying with joy. Then war intervenes.

Regression: Cliff's gone away, he's a pilot in World War I. I've been alone for a while, our child is growing.

Cliff's coming back now. I've waited so long. (She cries.) *I see him walking towards me, it's so good, we missed out on so much. He's battleworn, tired.*

Now our son's grown, he's got a lovely girlfriend, we're happy. But Cliff has chest pains. We're in our fifties.

We had another 20 years. I sit at his bedside, our son and his wife are there. Cliff tells me how much he loves me. He's going. I feel so lonely, I want to go with him.

Now I'm in my eighties, looking at a picture of Cliff when he was young. Pain in my chest, getting greater.

I'm on the floor. (She cries.) *Someone's taking my hand — Cliff's come to get me.* (She smiles.) *I'm going with him, he's young again.*

Coming back to herself — after Bettina comments that

Elizabeth's death pains in the chest seem connected with her current chest pains — she says, 'I still love Cliff now. We had some unfinished business. I want to be with him so badly, he must be my soulmate. It's as though he's a part of me.' Then as insights surfaced she said, 'Oh, oh — I see now. Between lives we planned to meet again this time.'

A week later she tells me that the crisis has passed. Where did the energy go? After releasing some stored pain, did her unconscious mind put this continuing love on hold for the future? She said, 'I feel more peaceful about my marriage now.' (And after exploring 12 past-life stories, she reported that her physical problems were also clearing.)

As Bettina was 26, it seems she reincarnated less than ten years after Elizabeth's death. In past-life tradition, fast return is the mark of a soul determined to progress quickly in Earth lessons. Many more individuals seem to be reincarnating fast as the pace of living and learning opportunities increases.

ANOTHER CHANCE

Happiness grabbed away by disaster in the distant past can be caught again today. A light-hearted young woman in a flow-ered bonnet and long dress, about to be betrothed, steps out from her eighteenth-century family's house, calling, 'I'm just going down to Mrs. Macy's shop.' It is a winter's morning. A horse-drawn carriage approaches, slides on icy cobblestones. Its panicking horses trample her to death.

Centuries later, a blonde teenager feels a special sense of rightness when she marries a man who reminds her of someone she can't quite identify. This bride is frightened of horses, but she doesn't know why.

A love affair springs up between a man and a woman who somehow feel familiar to each other. Investigating, they find they are completing what could not be completed before, when he was a mediaeval monk in a repressive sect, burned to death as an example, for enjoying conversations with a young woman. Months later the present couple separate. Has some deep need of the soul been satisfied?

A long-time husband who described his wife as 'really special' found that she was his twin in a past life. Her death separated them then. This time they shared life as intimates for many years.

Endless combinations of personal issues emerge when we examine love partnerships through the past lifetimes lens. Findings often explain difficult or puzzling aspects of relationships. Ideally, the techniques of this practice move us first to insights that bring reassurance and relief, and then beyond, to the deep energy shifts where change for the better occurs.

Not all past lifetime alliances are with loving soulmates. Anecdotal evidence suggests that any strong emotion held in other lifetimes may draw people together again, perhaps to work through old hatreds or guilts. Present partings may occur simply because couples do not know how to do this, or how to handle their present differences. They may find it easier to split, even if this prolongs grief, rage or bitterness.

GETTING CLEAR

Our best decisions come out of clarity, not out of emotional turmoil or blockage. In some marital situations, an avenue of help to the individual, if not necessarily to the marriage, is to gain clarity on centuries-old issues still active between present partners.

A man pondering his unsatisfactory marriage realises he is still with his wife because of a sense of obligation, apparently arising originally from a nineteenth-century life where he was a doctor who neglected his wife (his wife again now) in spite of, or because of, their ten children. He wonders if this past guilt played a part in his decision to marry her again. I suggest he clean up his distant past, that he finish the emotional business held over from the doctor's life story, so he can make clearer decisions in the present.

A woman separated from her husband feels he had been a mediaeval Roman Catholic torturer when she was a Cathar, whom he saw as a heretic. She sobs, 'He's still hurting me.' I encourage her to consciously complete with that life story through resolution work. From this she could find unsuspected strengths of her own to help in the present.

A woman now involved with a man who is cruel to her finds several past lives in which he has abandoned or killed her. As little change is evident, the obvious question is, 'How long are you willing to put up with this?' To help her to understand more, we explore what has happened in these stories, and apply present perspective.

Perhaps the ultimate in facing issues is to find that your live-in lover murdered you in a previous life. A man discovered through rebirthing that he had been a woman refugee in a world war. A Nazi soldier barred escape. Hoping to save her life she offered him sex, which he accepted. Immediately afterwards he said, 'I love you and I'm going to kill you.' He bayonetted her. Far from being upset, this client was excited because the events explained his present intimacy problems with his partner, who reminded him of the Nazi soldier. His psychic fear was already healing through present perspective. And he recalled that as an Australian child, he had been obsessed with war toys and love for Germans, although they were enemies at that time.

Karmic echoes can prevent a potential love affair from flowering. Perhaps from first sight, apparently irrational 'I don't trust you' feelings war with attraction, hovering below the surface like ghosts from the past — which they are.

The choices are to turn away from the relationship, or to go ahead in hope, or to work through this psychic static before it attracts proof. We may explore our most significant past lifetimes with such a person (whether or not the person knows this). When we have this overview from our own perspective, and have resolved whatever we can in the discovered situations — if our distrust is still present, perhaps it is valid. Obviously, not everyone is developed enough to be trustworthy, or truthful about change within themselves.

PAST LIVES SHOW A BIGGER PICTURE
Past-life work offers a wider picture of present issues.

A woman sees that in a past life she was her present lover's wet nurse, and also nursed him in his later invalid years. I ask if she is still metaphorically wet-nursing him, and if that is appropriate now.

A present lover is seen to be an attacker in a woman's past life. Today the issue is trust. She is nervous around him, finds openness and honesty hard. She now understands that her reticence had been a survival tactic in the past.

A woman finds that her former husband murdered her in another century. Has their time together in this century eroded that issue? Only if she can now feel easy around him. She doesn't. Even though they have parted, there is inner work for her to do to free herself, to avoid drawing to herself the same or another situation of aggressor and victim.

A woman was upset that a male friend would not feel passion for her. She quoted him as saying, 'It would kill me.' She found that it once had, when she'd knifed him in a crime of passion. They both had emotional completion work to do: she for her tendency to be deprived of a man she loved, he to un-learn that he had to be 'cut up' over love. The aim was not to create a love relationship, but to guide each individual to break old limiting patterns and so move forward safely.

REPEATING PATTERNS

Like the rest of us, you have probably moaned 'Oh, not again', as you find yourself in the same situation of embarrassment or frustration, or another dead-end love relationship. The men-are-bastards/women-are-bitches syndrome originates from our unconscious compulsions to relate to certain kinds of people we think we don't want, but can't keep away from. It's now known that often if ex-partners or children of alcoholics do not become alcoholics, they tend to marry in turn one or more alcoholics, although alcoholic addiction may not be initially evident.

We can also be addicted to negative emotional and mental patterns of life creation. 'Why?' we shout as we are once again devastated by being abandoned, betrayed, or violated — perhaps lifetime after lifetime: 'Why does this keep happening to me?'

Is it because we continually give ourselves new chances to wake up, to learn and grow? What old pain could we heal?

Guidance in such circumstances supports people through their distress and rage into increased understanding of themselves and of the other person. Then can come acceptance, or a better basis for decision-making, and perhaps, ultimately, forgiveness or love. Past selves are frequently useful allies in this, whether the traveller is working directly on a relationship with someone known now, or on the relationship with him or herself, which affects all other relationships.

One short cut out of emotional addictions is to identify the negative pattern in this life, focus our awareness on 'the past lifetime where this pattern began', explore this thoroughly, face its problems honestly, then process and resolve its issues within that life story.

In this way, we access the dynamics of our life energy at depths not normally accessible for healing. If we are willing to do this inner work even once, or more often, my experience shows we have a good chance of breaking the patterns.

In a culture where the divorce rate is climbing towards one in two marriages, such personal processing is becoming increasingly vital. Personal evolution is the process of first accepting, and then working to transmute, those emotions we so often try to reject.

The path to wholeness, according to American spiritual teacher Ram Dass, cannot be limited to the individual only, but is part of the evolution of the race. He sees spiritual work on ourselves as an offering to our fellow beings.

TRANSFORMATIONAL RELATING

The quality of relationship between lovers expresses the quality of life attracted by each individual. As we speak of a person in the process of becoming self-actualised, or whole, so also may we view a dedicated relationship. Now may be the first time in lifetimes of journeying together that a couple accepts what many couples today see as their deeper purpose in relating to each other. This is to support the other in developing wholeness, into evolving as an individual, rather than as a component of one unit, the relationship. When each wants only what is best for the other, sacrifice becomes obsolete.

A transformational relationship is a moment-by-moment adventure in which each loving partner opens more and more honestly to the other. Partners learn and grow together, continually revealing deepening layers of their inner being to themselves and to each other, sharing the gifts and trials of ever-increasing intimacy.

The idea — and ideal — is that with the person you love most, you continually open new doors within yourself. If this risk feels too uncomfortable to consider, it is likely that issues around intimacy are blocking your potential to be magnificently yourself, and therefore to manifest a magnificent quality of loving.

FOREVER RENEWING

Robert is a husband of 25 years, dedicated to both his own and his partner's continuing inner and outer development within a marriage that aims at being transformational. He says in delight, 'When I wake up each morning, this same woman beside me is always new !'

Robert and Gwen do not live in each other's pockets, but explore their joint and separate interests from a shared basis of deeper and deeper honesty about what is going on within themselves. A requirement for this goal is quality time spent alone together. Togetherness does not necessarily mean total agreement, nor does it mean only fused activities. Robert and Gwen are well aware that 'love brings up its opposite, for healing,' as international relationships teacher Sondra Ray points out. This means that the pressures of increased intimacy and caring push up unresolved issues.

While initially it may not be apparent, we often see that feelings and situations that appear in our primary relationships are feelings still festering from childhood between us and our parents. Instead of letting this kill the present relationship, we can take the opportunity to finish with these issues and let them go, through personal growth techniques, perhaps including past-life work.

Hopefully, we can have understanding and support from the partner who may be taking the brunt of the problem, yet who is at the same time confronting his or her own issues through the interaction. In this kind of relationship, neither partner says, 'It's my partner's problem, it's nothing to do with me.' The question becomes, 'Why am I relating to someone who behaves this way? What echo from the past is present in my own feelings?'

As this ideal of self-responsibility nurtures each individual above the relationship, it is a far cry from marriages that trundle along on the wheels of compromise. 'We never have a cross word,' the couple say. 'He has never raised his voice to me in 40 years.' The observer may ask - why not? What undercurrents of sacrifice and distortion, what strangled differences, are these people not dealing with? Peace at any price is an unhealthy situation. It's accepted today that continuing resentment can build arthritis, cancer and other crippling conditions. The compromise marriage deadens the life force of one or both partners. Its comfort is superficial and confining.

On the other hand, attempting to live out ideal relating is a never-ending challenge and not always comfortable. Besides joy, such a close partnership includes conflict, as well as its resolution. In their commitment to self-awareness, Robert and Gwen use truth-telling techniques for clearing issues as soon as they arise. These two believe that the bond between them is enriched through their having related before, in other lifetimes. Perhaps this gives them an edge of confidence to live this way now.

FEAR AND HURT

So often we settle for less because of fear in all its guises.

Pronounced fears of intimacy frequently arise from past experiences where intimacy has led to disaster. While we may not remember the origin of these fears, their influence reverberates in present attitudes. Fears operating in adulthood are usually rooted in childhood. Their tap roots may reach back through time to older learning.

But not all past-life learning is hallowed. In this life alone we have learned things that serve us and things that do not. Becoming conscious involves beginning to discern, and choosing again. Learning from experience can benefit us. But it can also shut us down if we get stuck in the belief that because things were once a certain way they will always be that way. Because we were once abandoned by a favourite lover in a past life — or in this life — we tend to 'learn' that all lovers will abandon us.

Some people fiercely resist love because of past hurt, and become unwilling to love at all. Experience shows that our pain and its accompanying beliefs, such as 'People I love leave me', or 'I don't deserve love', can indeed magnetise to us people who will abandon us, unless we break the chain by clearing out the effects of past unhappy situations.

Sometimes we get warnings that we are caught up in patterns. A woman's husband goes out to a meeting and never comes back — at the age her father was, when he went off to war and never came back. A man complains that when he was a boy his mother got sick and he had to cook; now his wife gets sick and he has to cook. What original incidents might these events be replaying? Would it serve these people now to go within and change the tape? A man regressing to a past self complains, 'My wife won't go out anywhere with me.' Neither will his present wife. Why has he twice, at least, chosen women who behave this way?

It seems that as the dramatic cycles of personal interaction spiral throughout one entity's lifetimes, over hundreds or thousands of years, major issues tend to lessen in force. After we have lived a number of lives on the same theme — perhaps of being attracted to people who don't value us — the issue may have worn itself out. This is unconscious learning.

Nowadays, if we choose to consciously deal with our problems, we not only accelerate progress in this life but hopefully avoid future pain that would have been caused by doing the same thing again. When we have mastered a lesson. we don't need to repeat it (perhaps not even in future lives). We go on to another lesson. In any life, learning gets easier with progress.

RAINBOW CORRIDORS OF TIME

Some of us keep wanting to know, 'But how can past life events influence us the present?' Suppose we looked at it this way.

In today's firming climate of energy field awareness, reincarnationally, human beings might be seen as rainbow lights dancing in an eternal parade, weaving multiple energy tracks down the corridors of time. We meet, blend, part and meet again, creating an everlasting tapestry of living light and colour.

This is not such a fanciful image. Traditionally, human energy fields, or auras, have been called 'light bodies'. The probing eye of science is now not only exploring these fields, but is also showing us that instead of being solid, our physical bodies — when viewed subatomically — are themselves made up of dancing energies. Particle physicists consider the smallest components of matter, for example, high energy photons or cosmic rays, to be particles of frozen light.

Colour is traditionally associated with the human energy field, as through the ages clairvoyant sight has sensed colours surrounding people — and Professor Hunt has explored this with electrical instruments. These colours are reported to vary with our state of being, according to emotions, health and spiritual development. Mystical teachings associate rainbow colours with the chakras. Early scientific investigation now suggests that chakras transmute the effects of higher vibrational inputs — possibly from Dr. Sheldrake's morphic fields — into biological manifestation, via our endocrine system. Chakras are also considered to be intimately associated with our emotional life.

Each human body, then, radiates its coloured energy field. Perhaps the auras of all our selves do indeed form rainbow corridors bridging time — along which coded messages travel. These messages are the major beliefs, or *samskaras* and *klesas*, that we carry from past lifetimes.

A love message from the past may be as simple as this one. Hundreds of years ago, a rural wedding takes place in a friendly community in the Scandinavian woods. Wedding bells peal, ribbons flash in the bride's hair, the groom wears his best brown boots. Then the couple walk alone to their new house under the trees. Here they live contentedly for 20 years, until the husband dies in a community raid on a neighbouring settlement.

From this scenario, today's individuals carry the message, 'Love is likely to end in grief, but it's worth the risk.' This is a happier conclusion than many we make. For example, 'I would die for love!' carries a ghostly implication that you once did, you have not let go of it, and so you might do it again, even if only metaphorically.

The positive messages we bring forward, such as, 'I always have the love I want', need no help to enrich our character and life experience. In a loving easy relationship, inner depths open up with past lifework, as each partner's understanding and appreciation of the other blossoms. But a message like 'Love hurts' can create pronounced fears of intimacy, and is surely worth healing.

Can you identify negative patterns in your present-life love relationships? Do you keep proving that 'I can't express myself with a lover', or 'Relationships imprison me', or 'I have to sacrifice myself to have a love partner', or any number of others?

Lovers can present us with our greatest life lessons. Self-transformation methods offer us ways to do something about these lessons. Otherwise we stockpile constricting beliefs that feel to us like the truth. We keep acting them out, but we can't understand why patterns repeat. More importantly — nor do we understand that we have the power to start changing this situation.

One way to undermine such unconscious blueprints is to experience impressions of 'the past lifetime where this pattern began'. Working with the characters in that story may well release the emotional charge holding the present pattern in place.

Past selves thereby demonstrate that they are not just static cut-outs from history. When we bring them to conscious awareness, we find that they are living energy fields intimately connected with our present. We may prove them to be valuable tools from our own consciousness for creating new possibilities now, even in our love life.

Chapter Four

Children and Other Relatives

An eight-year-old girl writes of a dream she names 'My Life Dream':

A long long time a go, i lived with a wondful young lady, her name was Alice. In that other life time Alice was my wife. In this life time Alice is my Mum.

She had golden hear and shining blue eyes. I met her in a deep but butiful forist. Alice loves nature. She abslotly adoors birds and animals and flours.

I was a wood cuter. My name was Edwin. I was a very inportend wood cuter. One day I went out to see a gleaming rubbit. It had little shining lites around it. Alice had found it.

All of a soden a 11 foot tree fell on me.

Alice was in her bed room getting puffed up (powdering her face) *and I was in the deepest part of the forist. Alice didn't hear me. It was 2 weeks before Alice found me and every day after she found me she yost to go into the forist and give me flours and every night I youst to go into her bed room and talk to her.*

About fifteen weeks later she had a baby girl and I was her baby girl. The End. P.S. Alice new that I, Edwin, was her baby girl.

This dreamer and her mother also live without a man in the house. Nature plays a big part in their lives but so far they have not found a rabbit adorned with luminous fungus.

Many, many children tell past lifetime memories spontaneously. Psychiatrist Dr Elisabeth Kübler-Ross told of a dying boy who comforted his distraught mother with the words, 'You're the best mother I ever had.' A six-year-old Australian girl who had always lived with her mother would periodically sleepwalk through the house calling for Mummy. Her mother would say, 'Darling, I'm here !' The child would say, 'No, not you. Mummy's left me !'

Mothers have told of a boy, 18-months-old, describing being in an air-raid shelter during the bombing of London; a two-year-old saying, 'I was your grandfather, before'; a six-year-old recounting life as a seaman on a sailing ship; a four-year-old pointing out, 'That's the church where I was buried'; a five-year-old refusing to fly in a plane because, she stated, she had died as a grown-up in a plane crash.

A man recalled being traumatised by a book he had seen at the age of nine, containing pictures of a beheading. 'I couldn't even go into the room where the book was,' he said. To release his phobia of beheading he had to wait many years until regression brought to light a guillotine experience in another life.

The mother of a 15-year-old boy wept with happiness after she regressed to a happy past-life childhood in a gracious house on a fine English estate. 'It gave me the answer', she explained. 'When my son was three, he said, "Mummy, do you remember where we lived before?" We'd always lived in the same house. But on that English estate, my son now was my beloved father.'

Children's remembered lives can affect not only their own outlook but also present family relationships. A listener to a radio talk told me that from the moment her daughter could speak she used to say, 'When I was your mother...' She added, 'She is very like my mother was. She tries to dominate us, she doesn't like the child role.'

Healing of difficult family situations may be advanced by invoking help from past-life stories to bring deeper understanding of the issues involved. For example, a parent's preference for one child above others, from the moment of the child's birth or even before, has been explained more than once by those two having been close in a previous life. They themselves may not realise or explore this possibility. But such a discovery by one sibling who had always felt left out eased the situation for him. It began to free him from the grip of long-held jealousy, founded in a fear that he was not as worthwhile a person as his father's favourite.

BARRIERS FALL BETWEEN LIFE STAGES
In the course of inner work, barriers between birth, life and death fall more easily for some people than for others. In his first rebirthing session, simply through undertaking conscious connected breathing with intent to improve his life, a business-

man relived being born into a primitive culture and also, in sadness, dying as that infant.

In a rapid series of impressions before and after the reincarnation incident, he spent minutes laughing, experienced his body as tiny and trapped in his present mother's birth canal, realised that she wanted to help him be born but was unable to, fell into grief for his present father who had committed suicide many years previously, and mentally communicated with an inner image of his father until joy replaced grief.

As he continued the breathing session with his eyes closed, the man said, 'I just had a talk with my (dead) mother. She's okay too.' Soon he said, 'She doesn't think too much of this exercise, says I should have known all this.' He laughed till tears rolled down his face: 'We're having a three-way conversation.' His father's contributions were predictably serious, but his mother was uncharacteristically laughing and swearing at him. When he finally wiped away tears of mirth, he had dropped the burdens of years — unresolved grief around the deaths of his parents, and previously unacknowledged sadness for himself — surfacing through a sad memory of his own past death in infancy.

REMEMBERING WOMB TENANCY

Not only are people proving they can remember birth, coming up with previously unknown facts that can be corroborated, but some people clearly remember more than one period of womb tenancy. It is usually the same womb. They seemed determined to get into a particular family.

A woman lying silently breathing suddenly sat upright saying, 'Oh, no!' She moved through distress, then began to breathe easily. Later she told me she had connected with being one of triplets in her mother's womb, before she herself was conceived. Two of the triplets had died in utero. She felt she had been one of them. The third, a boy, was born alive and was now her elder brother. She said, 'I hated him then because he went on into life and we died.' (Even that circumstance may echo rivalry in previous lives.)

These leftover feelings made sense to her. She had never understood why she disliked her brother so much. From that moment, their relationship was on a new footing, one she need not even explain to him. Understanding leads immediately to a lessening of tensions, thence towards new possibilities, even in the cases where massive past-life emotions underlie conflict with siblings or parents.

A teacher, Alan, re-experiencing during a rebirthing session being in his mother's womb, felt grief and loss and a sense that someone should have been in the womb with him. Later he rang his mother in another country and asked if he had been a twin. She said no.

A year later in another session Alan felt that he was in the womb with a twin brother, and that there was not enough life energy for them both. The other twin decided to die.

Alan said, 'I tried to lower my own metabolism to help him. But he died. I felt a sharp pain in my own body, then grief. Later I experienced myself dying in the womb.' That night, Alan's mother phoned him, saying she did not understand why, but earlier —- at the same time as his session — she had fallen into grief about twin babies Alan did not know she had miscarried before his conception. She had cried for two hours, tears that had been bottled up since one twin foetus had died at three months, the other at five months.

Alan had for some years been dedicated to teaching handicapped children. His driving spirit was to help children to whom the full life force is not available.

PATTERNS OF RELATING
In the course of regressions, shock recognition of individuals known in the present life is usually followed by moments of confusion, then relief, often accompanied by tears. A woman reports in amazement, 'I was my father's first wife, who died. No wonder I felt so close to him.' A man says, 'My sister shot me in a past life. I'm still angry at her!' A woman getting to know a new man friend is surprised that his teenage daughter immediately trusts and confides in her. She feels joy on discovering that the girl was her own beloved daughter in another life.

Another woman, struggling with lifelong difficulties with her sister, reports feeling better after realising in session that these difficulties are part of a long soul journey. She sensed that they had shared 68 past lives! And not all of those were as humans! (Regressions to 'one's first life on Earth' often reveal lives as animals.)

63

A woman obsessed with an apparently irrational fear of losing her 19-year-old son clears it through distant recall. We uncover a dramatic parting in ancient Rome, where they are also mother and son. At 19, the Roman son leaves her for an army career. The next time she sees him she is dying. After experiencing those long-ago emotions she finds her current fear has vanished.

SEEDS SOWN AROUND BIRTH

Anecdotes from inner travellers suggest that seeds of family relationships are set up as far back as birth and womb life, often following issues unresolved in previous incarnations. An interconnectedness among past and present lives, deaths, womb life and birth is becoming increasingly clear in transpersonal work.

As well, international scientific research over recent decades supports personal recall that babies sense something of the family dynamics even in the womb, possibly through identifying with the mother's feelings about family members and situations. As infants, we also imprint neurologically with gut level 'decisions' we make about those impressions with regard to ourselves, whether or not the impressions are related to fact. The nervous system is recognisable in an embryo 3 weeks old. The neural network and neuro-peptides are involved with memory.

Studies from medical and psychiatric research reporting on intelligent life in the womb — summarised by Dr Thomas Verny in the book *The Secret Life of the Unborn Child* — support the validity of foetal awarenesses and emotional states recalled by people in rebirthing sessions. The studies show undeniably that, from an early age, the foetus responds in its nervous system to core emotions such as love or rejection, and is influenced by the mother's thoughts, words, even hopes.

Such information travels from mother to foetus in three major ways, says Dr Verny: physiologically, especially through the mother's hormones; behaviourally, such as through the mother stroking — or not stroking — the foetus through her skin; and by sympathetic communication, which he defines as intuitive knowing.

Other findings from the scientific laboratory are that the foetus shies away from light as early as 16 weeks, responds to speech patterns at 20 weeks, and by six months is aware of the subtle shifts of the mother's emotions. The unborn child, states Dr Verny, feels, remembers, and is an extremely sensitive being. This intelligent awareness continues during birth, unless it is interrupted by anaesthetic.

Ultrasound scans support findings that babies have a mental and psychological life before birth, to the point that traumatic events such as threatened miscarriage seem to affect the foetus just as trauma after birth would, according to Italian researcher Dr Alessandra Piontelli.

Depending on both our mother's state of health and the degree of welcome and safety we sense waiting for us, as a foetus we may generally feel either secure or anxious, says Dr Verny. This foundation state resonates into our subsequent personality, as we become either a generally confident or an anxious person.

Foetal anxiety is illuminated in rebirthing when, for example, in working with people whose birth was late, the practitioner asks, 'Why don't you want to come out?' A common answer is, 'People will hurt me.' In many instances, such primal sensing also seems related to past-life and/or death memories of times when people did hurt them, as they report detail of what they sense happened in other lives. Such traumatic 'learning' predisposes people to distrust others this time, even other family members.

People may relive the first shock of infant imprinting with a lifelong negative pattern, a feeling that recurs under stress. 'I'm ugly', or, 'I hurt people I love', or, 'I'm worthless' are some of the core beliefs played out in the family environment, as we either prove the beliefs self-fulfilling, or go to great lengths to avoid proving them. Someone carrying a deep conviction of 'I'm unlovable' may become a people-pleaser to make sure nobody else discovers this 'truth'.

The discovery of perinatal imprinting as prototypic anxiety does not lay blame on parents, who are usually doing the best they can. But it does honestly reveal impressions that a baby gains. Both negative and positive impressions make an imprint, whether or not they are mistaken impressions. An imprint of 'I'm a delight to my parents' needs no healing. But every one of us carries some deep doubts or fears.

Metaphysically, we can see these are actually our tools for

learning, carried over from other life situations. For example, some people report that spiritual life lessons they need to learn around trust have brought them this time into families where others may not be trustworthy. One of the opportunities of the self-discovery path is to relive the start of such beliefs as 'I can't trust people', either during birth or during past lifetimes — because reliving begins release. In that case, release would mean that the untrustworthiness others had proved would either change, or would no longer victimise the individual who was clearing the emotional charge around the outlook.

CHOOSING OUR FAMILIES?
As fast as distant memories solve old puzzles, they may open up more, such as whether or not children choose their parents, and so choose their entire families.

Some of my clients have felt they recalled the act of choosing their parents before conception, in a realm of consciousness that seems to be *between* lifetimes. That choice is not affected by present feelings about their parents, they say, but relates to their sensed spiritual purpose in coming to Earth. A spirit wanting to learn more about self-respect may choose a family whose members constantly put down the human self, while another needing to learn more about strength may choose a childhood as the youngest, weakest sibling. The constant stress in such situations provides pressure to grow.

Pre-foetal spiritual choices appear to set up a resonance that directly affects future parents and relatives on Earth, who are usually — consciously — oblivious to this dimension, although it seems that at some level of consciousness the decision is joint. There are always lesson opportunities for everyone involved. We glimpse this when, as a foetus who died at birth, a woman feels she is hovering in spirit over the funeral of herself and her mother. She says, 'Oh! I see my next mother! I'll go to her because she loved my mother so much! This family needs me.' Born again, to her former aunt, the new baby forgets this for many years, until she has rebirthing sessions.

A thirty-five-year-old social worker who had never wanted to be a mother met a younger man. Three weeks later she said to him, 'I want your child. I don't mind whether you have any- thing to do with the child or not.' Two miscarriages later they married, and then had a son. Had they been influenced by the incoming spirit?

When this son could talk he looked down at a bush valley near their home and said calmly, 'I lived down there with a fat lady a long long time ago.' He also insisted he and his father had once lived in a cave, but his mother was not there. Imagination? Perhaps. This boy had a mother willing to listen. She did not admonish, 'Don't tell lies!' or 'How ridiculous!' Such a mother can say casually to a young child, 'What was it like in my tummy?' and get apparently genuine answers, such as 'Dark with bits of light.' Children are close to memories of earlier experiences.

NEW UNDERSTANDING

One of the many joys of past lifetimes work for the practitioner is to witness healings of the heart. Olga, in her forties, comes to me to improve her relationship with her father, who is in his seventies.

The father appears in a past lifetime as Olga's previous father who rejected her. Olga's past self yells resentfully at the past self of her father. (Olga says, 'I've needed to do that for a long time!') Even though in our first session Olga realises that she doesn't like her father, she reports that in the ensuing week their relationship is a little easier.

In the second session, after we had paved the way by clearing more past-life anger issues between them, I suggest Olga invite an image of her present father into her consciousness.

Counsellor	*Tell him honestly now what you feel and what you want.*
Olga	*He's not listening.*
Counsellor	*Make him listen. He's in your mental territory now.*
Olga	*'Stop talking, Dad, and feel for me occasionally!' You know, he's never said 'I love you', and I've never said it to him. I feel I should, but I can't.*
Counsellor	*Would you like to ask him why he hasn't?*
Olga	*He says, 'I never thought it necessary.'*
Counsellor	*If you'd like him to say it, tell him.*
Olga	*He's not too impressed — but he wants me to love him !*

Counsellor	*Explain to him why you haven't told him you love him.*
Olga	*'Dad, when I was young you didn't want me, and I knew it.' (The father image agrees, but wants to be loved.)*
Counsellor	*Would you like to ask him to say it?*
Olga	*'Dad, I want you to say you love me!'*

Olga reports that in her mind they are sitting talking at her dining table. I suggest that, because each of us tends to live in our private prison of limiting thoughts, old habits might be visualised as iron hoops around each person. Because she's dealing with her perceptions of her father, Olga has the power right now to lift those hoops off both of them. She does. She sighs. 'They've all gone! It feels good!'

Now the pair tell each other of their love, which has been hidden behind their differences. Olga is silent for some time, experiencing a profound change within herself initiated by her past self's screaming outburst at a father image. Before that, Olga had not seemed ready to express screaming outrage at her present father.

In the following week, for the first time Olga finds the courage to talk to her father about their love and their relationship. 'He's more open to me,' Olga says. 'But the main thing is, I feel peaceful around him.'

A grandfather is inspired to give his wife a birthday gift of a past lifetimes regression, although neither had ventured into these realms before. Her inner imagery puzzles her. She reports, 'They're wearing funny things', meaning foreign clothing. She experiences a richly rewarding story with her present beloved grandson, in another era. She scarcely believes the story, but leaves in a glow of wonder and smiles, feeling even closer to the boy.

A young woman wanting to heal her relationship with her present father reaches the truth of her anguish. 'Oh, Dad, all the lives we've had together, and we still can't show our love. Please Dad, love all of me, not just the bits that are like you!' Later she says, 'I feel calmer, as though I've resolved some things.'

LIVING IN THE PRESENT

We've all been hurt. In that sense, we can heal ourselves. Finishing with past situations enables us to live more fully in the present moment. We need to complete unfinished emotional business that stresses mind, heart, body, and sometimes spirit. Often we do not realise we are stressed by old emotions.

Close your eyes and think of someone who once wronged you. Now — when you think of that person, how does your body feel? What emotions do you experience? Listen to your thoughts. If that person walked up to you now, what would your reaction be? If there is any emotional charge — perhaps anger, tension, fear — you have not completed your interaction with that person, even if he or she is physically out of your life. You are clear only when you feel calmness, or mere preference, in relation to that person: 'It's fine to be with you now', or 'I'd prefer to be with someone else', rather than 'I can't stand to be around you.'

There is more to it than trying to force yourself to obey the injunction to love others, and probably feeling guilty when you can't. It is easy to fool yourself you have forgiven. There are steps to be taken to true forgiveness. *(See Chapter Six on 'Guilt'.)* One choice may be to explore the relationship in past lifetime terms. If the relationship is an important one, you may have been together before. Similar emotions will be present, and you may begin your healing work directly with the past-life character who triggers a charged response. Your present emotional blockage is significant enough to be echoed somewhere in your past lifetimes history, perhaps more than once.

Hanging on to old hurt makes you feel a victim. Incompleteness with other people blocks your love for yourself, as well as for them. The hurt was generated in the past. Yet although you may think you're over it, you still unknowingly drag it into the present. Your energy jams up whenever you bring the person to mind, or meet him or her — or meet other people who remind you of that person. Even similar situations can trigger the original discomfort you're still carrying around.

How can we check out when we have healed old emotional pain that has been interfering with feeling good about ourselves? We know, first of all, when similar hurt feelings do not arise now, even though we go openly into similar situations. Secondly, we are clear when we increasingly stretch past our old limits and enjoy more fulfilment in our lives, day by day.

HOW ABOUT KARMA?

In acknowledging hurt received or inflicted in the distant past, we are talking about negative karma. Karma is simply past conditioning, positive or negative. Traditionalists in reincarnation theory, such as Edgar Cayce, have taught that we are irrevocably tied to people we have wronged until we repay that debt. Today we can add, 'or until we choose to heal that situation'. American hypnotherapist Dick Sutphen claims that wisdom erases karma. Metaphysical teacher Louise Hay states that we can finish a karmic cycle whenever we choose, because the point of power is in the present.

If we happen to be acting out — living out — something as severe as deformity to 'pay' for past actions, I believe we can lessen even that stress if we are willing to do the inner work of facing, resolving and letting go. Past-life work holds promise, I believe, for new horizons in self-understanding for people of extremely small or large stature, people deformed, from whatever cause — in fact, anyone incapacitated yet able and willing to do the exploration. We are all more than our bodies.

But karma can be used as an excuse, a cop-out, for staying stuck in present circumstances when we could be resolving them and moving on. Perhaps you've heard something like, 'I have to be in pain now because I was cruel in a previous life', or 'I'm overweight now because I once starved to death', or 'I have to put up with being poor now because it's my karma.' With today's avenues for inner growth, we can answer, 'Great! Now that you know where it comes from, what are you doing about it?'

Negative karma is no longer a life sentence unless we choose to suffer from it. Hidden within it is always a vision of new possibilities.

FAMILY REJECTION

One aspect of negative karma might be to be part of a family that disturbs us, a family that metaphorically, as Woody Allen quips, breastfed us on falsies. Edgar Cayce has told us, 'Family is a river through which the soul flows'; each of us experiences that a family can be a smooth nurturing river — or a rocky cataract. Quite often people are so outraged by their family members that they fantasise they actually do not belong with them but were switched accidentally in the maternity hospital.

Steve used to comfort himself with this daydream during a lifetime of conflict with his parents and brother. 'I've disowned them all my life,' he said. In rebirthing, he discovered that he had imprinted at birth with the negative belief, 'I don't belong.' His greatest expression of this was within his family. As an adult, he had felt compelled to get away from them by leaving the country. In session, he was shocked to find himself in another lifetime with all his family members, who threw him out of a ninth-century family home. That self became a desolate wanderer.

In a sense, Steve had been repeating the past. Although he could see no change in the present character of his family members from the earlier story, he felt he himself had developed. He decided to work through his anger and bitterness, towards being able either to stay in the same country, or to leave freely rather than compulsively.

An outcast theme echoing through an individual's present life story might originally be of an abandoned child who steals, begs, and finally dies of malnutrition; a Muslim who offends his community's customs; a deranged woman sent away to roam a forest; a girl slave from a noble Roman household, sent to the lion pit because the staff quota of females is filled; or an Aboriginal man banned from his tribe because he will not kill or eat meat. Any of these individuals may have come into Earth life again as the two-month-premature baby whose gut reaction at birth, recalled through breathwork, was, 'I don't belong to the human race.'

It's possible that everyone who feels 'I'm a misfit' originally came to that conclusion in the present life through circumstances involving his or her birth. The imprint usually occurs when the baby is born to rejecting or ambivalent parents, but it can also happen straight after birth, as a reaction to separation from the mother in a hostile or depersonalised physical environment. The gut feeling then becomes a part of the individual's attitude to life, and sooner or later seems to prove itself repeatedly.

As a deep-seated suspicion or conviction, 'I don't belong' is not only the prerogative of compulsive travellers and derelicts. An early researcher into the importance of birth in character

71

formation, British psychiatrist Dr Frank Lake, found that even people in close family situations may be stressed by this anxiety, and behave so as to avoid proving it, although they may never tell anyone. In past-life counselling, an opportunity exists to find the distant origin and heal it, thus dropping the misfit feelings that influence the individual's behaviour.

CHILDBIRTH AND PAST LIFETIMES

Increasingly, mothers-to-be are being drawn to meditational contact with the growing child within them. In the special state of consciousness accompanying pregnancy, women are often wide open to intuitive knowledge about their babies. If a woman senses previous closeness in past lifetimes, this can immensely enrich the pregnancy and birth experience for both mother and child. Even if any conflict from those times should come to mind, there is opportunity for a heart-to-heart 'talk' — in visualisation — with the incoming baby, to make peace.

In early labour, the mother who is allowed to stay privately with her own process can spontaneously connect with previous lives, and previous births, as part of the rich experience that natural childbirth can be.

In labour one woman 'saw' a 3000-year montage of giving birth and being born, stretching back to ancient Egypt. This imbued her with an overwhelming sense of spiritual connection, deepening the conviction of sacred rite in which her body was embracing and giving life to her new baby. She felt she had already regularly communicated with the incoming spirit, felt she understood something of their shared life lessons to come, and was able to give, and receive, inner reassurance during his birth journey.

Another mother had to wait 20 years to understand why she had recognised, and felt guilty towards, the baby son she held in her arms for the first time. 'I knew we were playing the next round,' she said, 'but I couldn't understand it. In a recent regression I recognised him as someone I had harmed, before.' She realised that, by then, her devoted mothering had made it up to him.

Before his pregnant wife had a miscarriage, a father dreamed he met the incoming being. He saw him as an entertainer, an acrobat, a dwarf. Did this father sense a previous incarnation of the foetus, or was the foetus indicating that it was dwarfed, or both?

A CASE OF FAMILY TREACHERY
In seeking to release panic attacks, Elise found herself dealing with treachery from her parents in a past lifetime. As we worked, it became evident that a component of the panic attacks was unfinished business with her present parents. In both lifetimes the parents are fundamentalist Christians, unsympathetic to their daughter's differing points of view.

Regression : (A French teenager, Annabella, disregards instructions from her repressive parents not to go outside their gate. Joyfully she picks flowers in a field, but says:)
I'm running, shouting. Something is after me — a bear ! I'm on the ground, I can't move. It's dark, heavy, its face is so close to mine, a warm smell. It's looking into my eyes, it wants to kill me. I'm petrified.

I'm unconscious now. It's left me. I can't move. Bumpy — I'm in a cart, a brown horse pulls it. I'm being saved, but I'm so broken. I see an old woman hunched over in brown robes. She puts me to bed, tends me with herbs. My body is twisted, deformed.

But I'm smiling now, I'm lucky to be alive. I live with her, my parents didn't want me back now I'm ugly and one shoulder's higher. She's taught me a lot, I look after little animals.

Now I'm sad, someone's dragging me away. Men around me wearing helmets with nose protectors, and metal armour. They can't understand. They think we're witches or something.

I'm tied to something, burning to death, the fire's consuming my feet and legs, climbing up. I'm burning, it's so unfair. The pain. I'm confused. The old woman's watching, she's sad. They burn her as well, next. That's my fault.

Oh, oh, it's all my parents' fault. They thought I was evil because I was deformed. They're ugly, twisted. They said, 'The Devil's in you', telling me they had to do it for the sake of my soul.

I'm so angry with them. I want to leave my body so that I can haunt them for the rest of their lives. I do. I make sounds like dragging feet and chains for a long, long time, even after they die. But they didn't understand what a terrible thing they did to me.

73

Weeks later Elise said, 'Working with that lifetime enabled me to drop a lot of anger, bitterness and resentment I had towards my parents in this life, for emotionally crippling me. I used to limit my contact with them but recently I just welcomed them with open arms. I felt like being more interested in them, even though I couldn't tell them about the past life, they'd have been upset. And for the first time, they asked me for help.'

Historically true or not, past-life stories conceptualise our current challenges. We use them as symbols to transform and release new energies.

And if they are symbols, or metaphors, of what is going on in our consciousness — is our present life also a symbol?

If so — of what? And for whom?

Chapter Five

Self-confidence

Dream reported by Brad, a city security guard:

It's so vivid, the Clydesdale horses, two cows, I'm bartering corn, leeks, potatoes, rhubarb, I've made my own cheese, I'm at the local inn. Could I really have been a farmer?

Regression: *A good harvest, wheat and corn. A group of eight friends on a dray, there's a woman with a scythe. Now I'm at a market. Now I'm ploughing.*

I'm 43-years-old, standing on turf, wearing sandals and a brown tunic with a wide leather belt, nothing underneath it. Maybe my name is Turf. I'm very blond, my hair is spiky like hay, a round happy face. What I most love to do is eat lunch, cheese and bread, at my house. I also like to walk at night through my fields, I love to feel the wheat rubbing on my skin. Horses in a barn. Eight chains of land, left to me by my father.

My childhood in London was good, going to the sea to look at ships, but if I got married I'd want something substantial, a strong structure over our heads. I have it now, I built it, the innkeeper taught me to build.

Now I have a wife, she worked at the inn, came from Southampton. The first time I saw her she brought us more ale. I tell her I'm lonely, she says she's lonely too, she'll come and see me at my farm. She's brought a live duck, it's squawking, she puts it on the table, a present. She's offered to come and work with me, to cook and start off pigs and vegetables. I didn't know what it would do to me. After she left I sat up with my parchment and pen and candle and wrote down all the good things I could do, and all the problems she'd cause. The first time we made love was good, I'd never experienced anything like that before.

We're at the market, I wear an aqua-blue tunic and a green scarf and leather thongs, she wears a blue-and-parchment-coloured dress. What can we get in barter? A cross-saw to cut up fence posts. The market's very noisy. There's children squealing at a jester juggling little potatoes, he wears a tunic in coloured squares with hide moccasins. There's an axe-throwing competition, the target's on a tree. People row on the river. A competition to find the strongest horse, tie a piece of vine around the horse with a marker on the ground. Jan's looking at the weaving and yarning, I feel close to her.

My biggest problem is a flood, rain, all the chalk in the plains is coming up with the roots of the wheat, white and muddy underfoot, my crops will be destroyed. The land is flat, lots of water on it, an underground river.

My religion? I worship the ground, that's where my sustenance comes from. The village has a white stone church on a hill, a Druid priest who's also a farmer, we worship the Earth God. A ceremony worries me, sacrificing a lamb for a good harvest, it's not right, we're not a bloodthirsty people.

It rained into the brown earth, the corn is yellow and green, the wheat so beautiful it seems to be talking to me, it's so very happy that the Earth and the water have helped it grow, it wants me to start a bakery and make bread with it.

When Jan says she's having my child I am so excited I go out and plough the field at night! I worry for her, 'Don't work in the fields.' Now I'm asleep on the floor on my corn mat, the earth floor's warm. Jan screams, it's time. She's strong but the tension's too much for me, I go for a walk in the rain, when I come back I've got a son! So small, crying, Jan's crying too, she's so pleased for me. I hold him in a calico blanket. (Brad weeps with joy.)

My son has a lashed crib with straw and corn in the bottom. Jason! Neighbours come with fruit and baskets of lovely brown eggs. Now I have a son who'll grow strong and help me get more fields and lots of cows. We have ale and raw carrots and lots and lots of lovely creamy cheese, thick slices of bread. My butter, bread, cheese and milk! I'm so happy.

Me and my friends go into the barn and sit around a fire, it's raining, we spill ale all over our tunics, drunk and happy.

On the last day of my life I sit with my son in my field, he's 12. I'm very sad because I know I'll die soon. I've taught him my trade, my son feels like me. I tell him to look after the farm and his mother. Now I sit at my table, there's a sheaf of wheat on it. I feel very warm, the Eternal Spirit is in my body. Jan doesn't know.

I die in Jan's arms, she cries an awful lot.

I had everything I wanted, I enjoyed life. I'm in silver light, I just want to be by myself for a while, I've had people around me all my life. The life lesson was, I was good enough to be able to manage, to do things with my hands, and get results.

Brad was so moved by this experience that he began talking about taking his holidays on a farm.

He's big, tough and good at his job although often stressed. His relationships with women had been painful, and he was single. His colleagues and customers didn't have time for emotions or dreams. Yet he was open, and when a long-ago farmer tapped at his dreams with a message that his mental and emotional health required more contact with Nature, he listened.

Every event of that life story boosted his confidence in his practical abilities, his capacity to enjoy being a husband, father and provider for the community.

FORGOTTEN HAPPINESS

Our soul history is a storehouse of forgotten treasures. Contacting a forgotten happy lifetime can not only be a joyful experience, but can also release a source of unexpected strength into the present.

A young woman called Rhonda needed an influx of confidence when she became stressed by competition for promotion within a computer firm. 'I know I'm a good person,' said Rhonda, 'but deep down, I've always suspected I'm worthless.' This was a surprising statement. She is attractive and earning good money. 'That feeling is only something you've learned,' I assure her. 'What's learned can be unlearned.'

From interviewing her, I suspect that her secret feeling of worthlessness is a misunderstanding she arrived at as an infant, before she had any reasoning power. Yet it is too late for mere verbal reassurance to change this belief. The sabotaging thoughts, with their attached feelings of shame, hopelessness and self-blame, surface from deep in her psyche whenever she is under extra pressure.

Rather than go immediately to heal the past lifetime where she first 'learned' worthlessness, I direct her to a strengthening lifetime. The story that makes her smile throughout is of Ingrid, a happy European wife and mother living on a beautiful farm near mountains, by a village, centuries ago. Ingrid and her husband work hard, have five children and many friends.

She loves to go for walks under the mountains. At 76, she's contented, in good health, surrounded by family, and recalling events of 'a simple, good life'.

After Rhonda separates from Ingrid she still feels warm and happy. She likes Ingrid, and appreciates her competence, her value to family and village, and how well loved she was. Somehow Ingrid's confidence seeps into Rhonda at a deep level of consciousness, although the story itself recedes in a week or so.

As with Rhonda, appearances can conceal the state of our self-esteem. Another woman, beautiful, fashionably dressed, warm-hearted and sensitive, confides sadly, 'My husband deserves better than me.' And Alan, a widower of middle years, has hidden his anxieties all his life behind a confident facade. After embarking on a personal growth program, he begins to deal with the truth of his anxiety state, saying. 'I used to think the past was past. Now I know that's not so, it needs cleansing.'

If we often get caught up in feeling too sad, frightened, self-critical, guilty or anxious to feel good about ourselves, we can do something about this. We can make an effort to reconnect with a period in this or another lifetime when we did feel the glow of self-esteem, the glow of loving ourselves — and keep bringing those feelings into our present. From my experience, most people can recall one or more past lives where they demonstrated qualities and abilities they feel they lack now: courage, talent, leadership, confidence, assertiveness, capability or value to other people, which in other lives proved to be well founded because of the past self's achievements.

In each of our lives, it seems that we can take on so much challenge that we forget some things we've already learned. To use self-esteem as an example, perhaps some of us forget our inherent value on purpose — so that we can explore more deeply into other facets of being that may not be so available to a consistently high achiever. We might be able to explore, say, our sensitivities and spirituality more deeply when we are not wholly focused on the rewards of material success.

But ultimately, the drive for wholeness integrates all our strengths.

Up to now, perhaps for millions of Earth years, we may have lived all of our lives on a plane of unconscious learning:

groping around in the darkness of unknowing, not realising we were here to learn, not knowing what to learn, nor how to learn it. We were not born with a guidebook to being human in our hand. As someone has observed, our job seems to be to write the guidebook. Past lives provide its illustrations.

Picture a simple-minded man born in a Balkan city a few centuries back. His mother cares for him throughout his childhood, and his adulthood also. Each day she takes him from their small home to sit on a grubby bag and beg in the marketplace, where he can watch, hear and smell the crowds. He is an appreciative but passive audience to the multicolored bustle of activity and entertainment that is different each day.

This solitary man has a minimum of self-confidence, although he seems content. He is incapable of taking action. Eventually he dies, regretting that he did not make any lasting contribution to the world. He would like to have carved beauty into wood for some great church.

Yvette, the woman who discovered she knew that man intimately, out of her own past, lives her own life in a constant whirl of action. She does only things she loves to do, does them well, equally for herself and for others. She is a dynamo who juggles family, house, three part-time careers, continuing education for herself, citizen activist programs, sports, parties, concerts and travel. Two of her careers are concerned with children who are in some way damaged or disadvantaged, as her past self had been. She is also an artist, happily creating artwork for generations to come.

Even before Yvette discovered this past lifetime, she knew she wanted more out of life than sitting around all day! She does not believe in reincarnation, but she honours the power of the story.

SELF-FULFILLING BELIEFS
Our present-life memories are selective. People with high self-esteem remember instances of inspiring support from people around them in childhood. People with low self-esteem are likely to recall some horror stories from their childhood, of someone older or bigger saying or doing something from which they decided they were not good enough. And lessons like that can be so extremely painful that people push them into the subconscious. Yet their results continue.

As children, we are vulnerable to parents, grandparents, teachers, friends and siblings, all of whom have many ways of driving home negative messages: 'You'll never amount to anything!', 'There's something seriously wrong with you!', 'You stupid child !', 'You're useless!', 'Monkeyface!' Can you add messages you received that could have affected your self-confidence? Did all your family members always greet you with 'Hello, Beautiful!'?

The beliefs we adopt are self-fulfilling. They seem truly the way life is, because we constantly seem to be proving them. Negative beliefs sap our spirit as well as our self-esteem. To break the spell of such learning, we need to discover the negative belief, then face and fully embrace our feelings about it as often as necessary. This will begin to dissolve it, as truth is a powerful healing factor. We may need to do personal growth work to accelerate the letting-go. When our life starts proving the opposite of the negative belief, we are free. Life gets easier. We have more energy to flow into the positive, and to deal with the next emerging step of growth.

Past-life stories can point up deep self-doubts we may never have acknowledged to anyone, for healing. Such buried feelings make life harder under stress.

An executive in a high-stress job said spontaneously during a rebirthing session: 'I keep on seeing this desert, and I've never been there — not a good feeling — loneliness — it's like dying, I'm a baby — I can see a woman's feet, young, grey-black skin — she dropped me there — I've just been born — now I'm dying — I was useless, because she couldn't feed me.' Next time he's under stress, when he suspects he is useless, he can send that thought back to where it probably began. This man has also contacted its present-life trigger, of feeling useless during the rigours of his own birth.

MASTER JUDGEMENTS

As discussed earlier, our major self-doubts are now being shown to begin sometimes even before birth. About 40 common master judgements people begin making against themselves during infantile stress before, during or just after birth, have been identified by pioneer rebirthers, through people's experiences in sessions. It seems probable that everyone identifies with one or more of these, which are far stronger for some people than others, according to the supportiveness or otherwise of subsequent parenting.

A common underlying feeling is 'I'm not good enough.' A number of clients have told me, 'People leave me because I'm not good enough.' Often when we feel not good enough we also feel our home is not good enough, our work, clothes, ideas, even our friends and relatives are not good enough. A man explained, 'When people say they love me, I think they're not good enough.'

This, and other judgements, such as 'I'm a nuisance', 'I can't get started', or 'I'm ugly/dirty/messy/stupid', may affect a tiny part of a life, or they may overshadow the whole, even to the point of suicide, whether or not they are recognised as perinatal neurological imprinting. Experiencing ourselves differently in non-ordinary states of consciousness, as we do in rebirthing and past-life work, proves that however real these negative thoughts seem, they can be changed.

One woman who felt worthless was conceived when her mother was only 16. Parents pressured the pregnant teenager to marry the father although she did not want to. Two decades later in a breathing session the woman recalled her gut response as a foetus to impulses of rejection pouring into her from her mother: 'It must be my fault, or else she'd want me. I must be unlovable.'

This woman, who as an adult felt unlovable, connected in session with her teenage mother's desperate wish to abort her. The foetus reacted with terror and the desire to hide. No wonder the woman had gone through life unconsciously wanting to be unobtrusive! Being present had once been life-endangering.

Yet her low self-esteem can also be tracked back further. This mind-set is likely to be a continuation from generations of physical ancestors doubting their self-worth, as well as from psychic ancestors with low self-esteem. Finding and demonstrating confidence is clearly her spiritual task in this life — to break these patterns. In her sessions she was releasing deep-seated stresses that had been holding them in place.

As researcher Dr Verny informs us, evidence is mounting that among the things a baby senses before birth is not only its own sex but whether one or both parents really want a boy or a girl. If the baby is of the desired sex, he or she can begin life feeling secure. If not, the baby's gut reaction can be 'I'm wrong' or 'I'm the wrong one' or 'There's something wrong with me.'

This can be embodied later as gender confusion, and tracked back further to relevant past lifetime issues.

Women have reported memories of being fearful of their approaching birth into a family of brothers. While it is likely that a foetus may absorb fear of males from the mother, some women have substantiated this with past-life stories of terrifying persecution by men. They have started life this time feeling physically inferior and threatened, rather than confident.

An attractive woman recalled being stuck from the waist down in her mother's body during birth, afraid to reveal that she was the 'wrong' sex. This feeling had undermined her confidence in her femininity throughout her life until she discovered it and began to resolve it.

She has also connected with past lives involving punishment, or penalties, for having been female. This reflects historical truth on a massive scale, and is familiar to the past lifetime practitioner. Even today, according to Amnesty International, millions of women are mutilated, battered to death, burned alive, bought and sold as slaves. Most of the world's poor, and 80 per cent of war refugees, are women and their dependent children. Such stories surface from the far memories of women today — and are also past lifetime memories for some men.

'I'M BAD'

Many people's confidence is undermined by deep-seated feelings of 'I'm bad' or even 'I'm evil'. Sadly, this is not uncommon among children adopted at birth. Reports of recall claim that the foetus senses the coming abandonment before, during and after birth, and at gut level blames itself. I have witnessed such recall many times.

The good news is — such recall is a forerunner to dealing with this imprinted sense of abandonment. It can even lead to a person's ultimate forgiveness of the mother who felt she had to give up her baby. Such forgiveness reverberates into more self-confidence in the present, flowing into relationships with people such as love partners, friends or business associates whom the adopted person has unconsciously viewed as representing the abandoning mother.

An adopted boy I met as a handsome teenager was troubled by horrifying dreams. His unconscious infantile decision of 'I'm bad' had been strengthened when his adoptive parents had recently told him he was the son of a prostitute. His fears came to awareness in the dreams, which were a safety valve, and may have prevented him from unknowingly attracting life events to prove his thought that he was bad.

'I'm bad' surfaced in session for an adopted Australian girl, whose life circumstances as a teenager seemed to her to keep proving this. She had grown up with parents who kept telling her she was a bad girl. In her case, a few sessions of past lifetimes release on this theme were only a beginning in erasing that negative learning. Her body was suffering cancer; it had literally 'gone bad'. Yet sessions brought the belief into clear focus through several powerful stories that she was able to resolve. She could then begin to view 'I'm bad' as the belief it was, rather than a fact.

(Differing scenarios emerge around past lifetime origins of adoption in this life, showing sometimes a continuation of other lifetimes of conviction of 'I'm bad', or stories in which the past self has abandoned children. I believe such potentially painful material is best handled with professional support.)

An 80-year-old woman vividly recalled that as a two-year-old (in this life) she'd decided that she must be bad. She said, 'I was perched on a wall in the garden. I was desperate. I felt that "the others" had gone on and left me behind — so I must be bad. Who were "the others"? I don't know.' Spirit friends? Companions in the nursery of her maternity hospital? She felt she had spent her life trying to disguise the 'truth' of her 'badness'.

Probably her parents' disciplinary methods compounded her feeling of 'I'm bad'. We might think twice before we smack our children and say 'Bad boy!' or 'You bad little girl!' Are we programming them to act out just what we don't want?

What is the answer then, for children who become convinced they must be bad because of adoption rejection, sexual abuse, neglect or any other hurtful experience?

While positive verbal support can help, even professional assistance in releasing master judgements needs to go beyond words, to experientially reach the depths in consciousness and within the nervous system where the original hurt has been imprinted. The eradication of these feelings requires in-depth personal growth work later in life.

But parents aware that a child may be carrying such thoughts can counteract them by often including an opposite word, such as 'good' or 'valuable', in their praise of the child.

Discovery of the belief is the first step. If the people quoted above had been motivated or supported to do clearing processes perhaps in their teens, would growing up and life itself have been easier? An emerging preoccupation with self-development and self-healing in sections of society indicates that next century this could become an early life option, as normal as vocational guidance.

PAST LIFETIME CONDITIONING

Many people imprint in infancy with a belief 'I'm worthless,' especially if one or both parents don't want a child. These people are likely to discover that this belief began in previous existences. Master judgements may all be traceable to previous lives, where healing can begin.

Sometimes we 'learn' that we are not valuable human beings through traumatic incident during a past life or around a past death, or through circumstances that lasted a whole lifetime in the past. Some stories seem like templates for worthlessness. Consider how you might feel about yourself now, if you had been:

* an only child of six living in a mediaeval cottage deep in a forest, whose parents rode away in a horse-drawn cart and never returned.

* an English girl in the thirteenth century, sold as a servant at the age of five.

* a five-year-old boy stolen from his parents' Mediterranean vineyard by a pirate, sexually abused, then killed.

* a bewildered seven-year-old hiding under a guillotine platform during the French Revolution, while her parents above were beheaded to the cheers of the crowd.

* a slave boy who, placed in an orphanage at three and made to work in cotton fields at seven, became ill in the fields and was whipped to death by an overseer shouting abuse.

* a solitary, unwanted, mute child of 12, whose greatest pleasure was watching a courtyard fountain forbidden to her, battered to death by a beer-drinking companion of her mother.

These stories were all surprises to the people who recalled

them, and so were the accompanying tears. Whether or not the stories are true, the emotions are authentic. 'Where did those feelings come from?' people often ask in amazement. The feelings are our own repressed feelings, brought to the surface by the personalised story.

'The only touching in our family was hitting,' says a man of his childhood in this life. Being beaten in a past life also can hammer in feelings of worthlessness. An echo from the past is sixteenth-century Mary, from an Irish family of eight, forced to leave home as a teenager because there is not enough money. She goes to England, becomes a servant to an English farmer, and loves a poor man who is executed for theft while she is pregnant to him. She is thrown off the farm as 'useless', abused as a slut by local people, and finally beaten to death by strangers.

Some people avoid intimate relationships because of deep feelings of inferiority. A pretty woman, who secretly feels she is ugly, relives being a lonely man in an Islamic country. All his life he feels ugly, worthless and stupid, and dies unhappily in disgrace. As we explore further, the woman discovers that brutal treatment from the father in that life caused the man's low self-esteem. She is able to 're-educate' this past self (and herself) towards feeling worthy to share love.

We see that life lessons such as these can have such a deep impact that they influence us over hundreds of years. But their emergence into awareness means that, automatically, their emotional charge begins to dissipate. Negative conditioning is most powerful while we are unconscious of it. When simple techniques are applied to past lifetime situations in a safe environment, the memories can quickly lose power and become ordinary. By resolving the past-life issues, we help damaged parts of ourselves. We free up vital life energy that then directly nourishes a formerly doubt-laden self image.

THE EVER-CHANGING PRESENT

Because Rhonda visited her past for release from feelings of unworthiness, the energy of a contented farmwife and mother — the long-dead Ingrid — is now supporting Rhonda to develop her emotional skills. Ingrid's experience is also strengthening Rhonda's capacities for bonding with others in group situations, either of blood ties or of shared values. These are invaluable gifts.

But they may be all that the past self can give Rhonda, because of the differences in their Earth timing. Ingrid was confident in her own unchanging rural environment, where the adventure of the year might have been a trip to the saleyards. She knew her place, her family lineage, who she could depend on, what her behavioural boundaries were, and what she might expect out of the kind of life that had been repeated for many centuries. And she knew she was loved.

Do you know who you really are? And where you belong? Is your life as simple and ordered as the life of this woman of earlier times? Today's mobility, fractured family networks, and kaleidoscopes of change in the workplace and among friendships present us with constant challenges. In order to build up a support system of the kind Ingrid had, many of us must start among strangers. Even people nested into family structures seldom find such peace as Ingrid knew. The higher expectations and the many more choices available in the current Age of Information bring increasing conflicts as well as benefits.

Sometimes mere discovery of our karmic steps to now can ease pressure on current situations, allowing new possibilities to emerge.

Estelle, facing a new lifestyle with trepidation, met a past self with so many resources of eloquence, ease in public and loving-heartedness that she changed her first name to that of the past self. She knew that from then on, each time anyone called her by the new name, the powerful warm feelings and confidence she now associated with that name would vitalise her afresh. And so it happened.

The story faded but its inspiration lived daily. She did not try to live the reality of the past self. She took the gifts and integrated them into her present life — even though she wondered if the lifestory were true.

Courage to stand up for herself in an office situation was Cheryl's need. She was intimidated by a supervisor who she felt victimised her. She said, 'I want to find a past life where I had some authority. I know it's in me.' After regression she was solemn and wide-eyed.

Cheryl had experienced one of the marvels of past lifetime journeying — exploring how it feels to be of the opposite sex. Cheryl had met herself as a man of commerce, who dealt so wisely and kindly with townspeople that he was awarded great honour.

86

I asked what resource this self could give her to help her at work. She said immediately, 'His gift of understanding.' She decided that when she felt menaced by the supervisor she would choose to re-experience the calmness and stability this man had brought to her across the chasm of centuries. She reported later that it worked, and that she could now regard the supervisor as less of an ogre, more of a fellow human being.

ASPECTS OF SELF-CONFIDENCE

A number of lives attracted another woman's attention in her search for self-confidence.

One revealed a Scandinavian skin hunter named Raastas, who, in hard times, took weeks to work up the courage to steal a money purse, to buy food for his wife. He was caught, put in stocks and left in the snow, prey to agonising attacks by passersby and wild animals, until he died days later.

Throughout his ordeal, Raastas felt enraged at the injustice of his punishment. He felt hugely misunderstood. Marni, the seeker, often felt misunderstood, which undermined her confidence.

She then contacted a life where she had been understood. She says: 'I found myself as a man nicknamed "The Joker". He was full of confidence, but it was a manipulative, arrogant kind that brought him no personal satisfaction. People understood him alright. But I learned that being understood does not necessarily ensure self-fulfilment.

'Then I explored the life where I had the most confidence. Once again, it did not bring me any great joy. I was an intimidating, powerful and wealthy Dutch businesswoman in the eighteenth century. Her mistrusting and impatient nature resulted in a lonely and bitter life. She needed to have her heart in her affairs. So I learned that there's a lot more to confidence than just being assertive and self-assured.'

Marni said she herself expressed her lack of self-confidence by 'freezing up' in a group situation (Raastas died cold), and by being too opinionated in one-to-one encounters (like the Dutch woman).

She had wanted to understand why, when people focussed on her, she suffered so much anxiety. She explained, 'An answer lay in two past lives, where my being the source of attention brought me great suffering and death. First was Raastas, whipped and left to bleed to death in public, scavenged by wild animals. And there was a second life when I was burned at the stake in front of a crowd. Reliving these lives helped my self-confidence, but not enough.

'I found three others, all revolving around having to prove myself to a group of people. First, I was a mediaeval boy soldier who lost his nerve in battle. I willingly allowed myself to be killed in order to escape facing my fellow soldiers. In the second, I failed a tribal test of manhood and was ostracised by my community. In the third, in ancient Mesopotamia, when I craved to be accepted by the priesthood of a sect, I hysterically failed the first initiation test. I was so humiliated that I shunned my community, living out my days in my family home. Is one of the reasons I have returned to this Earthly plane the need to test myself in front of others?

'A lesson underlying all the past lives I've recalled seems to be, "Be true to yourself". Looking at these lifetimes throws clarity on the concept of the soul's voyage of self-discovery, using different possibilities of time and space — so simple, yet so complicated. What a paradox!'

A month later when I asked her, 'How's your self-confidence?' Marni looked surprised. 'H'm,' she said. 'It used to be such a big deal that I was obsessed with it. Now I hardly ever think of it. So I guess it's improved a lot.'

LIFE CHANGE CRISES
Crises associated with age milestones can throw up feelings intensified by past-life situations.

Puberty, fraught with change and discomfort, may stir such echoes in time. By 13 Shirley, self-conscious, plump and retiring, is convinced she is ugly. Seven years later, she discovers a past-life image of ugliness deep in her consciousness. A hundred years ago in England, a girl child is born with a disfigured face, and kept in isolation all her life by parents ashamed of her. Finally, in early teens, she is taken out into the woods one night and secretly killed. So, added to Shirley's conviction of ugliness, has been unconscious 'knowledge' that the penalty for ugliness is isolation and death. That is not a recipe for confidence.

Mid-life crises can also throw up depths of misery that seem out of proportion to the present. Bill, a musician in his forties, becomes convinced that he is a failure. In fact, he has had many successes but has always stopped short of big commercial success.

We find five lives in which his past selves are convinced they have failed. The first self to tell his story, of a fatal error of judgment, died at the age at which Bill's feelings of inadequacies are now peaking. As we work, the stories trigger strong body sensations and emotions in him. He is peeling off layer after layer of unconscious conditioning to feel a failure. (A few years later, he wins a big money lottery.)

Our past selves could be adding their weight of nervousness and negative beliefs to any difficulties we have with self-confidence in the present. The good news is, that such a discovery may bring with it a way out of the problem.

Chapter Six

Guilt

Barry, a young musician, seeks an answer to 'Why did I have a Caesarean birth?':

Regression *I'm between lives. There are people telling me that I have to have a violent birth. It's like a magnet. I feel it's right but I'm frightened. I have to learn the physical body isn't everything.*

Now I'm a man, a barbarian, really blond hair. Wow, so aggressive. My name is Azgar. My speech is guttural, like a noise, the sounds are unintelligible but the meaning is, 'Look how strong I am !' My mother was really rough. When I was adolescent she killed my father while they were making love. He was a bastard, he kept telling her she was no good at sex, she got sick of it.

I've got a broadsword, like an axe. I'm hacking people to pieces, I'm so strong ! I'm laughing. Women, men, children — IT FEELS GREAT! I'm in a place full of big columns, dead people everywhere.

(Barry says, 'It's Rome.') *Really developed people think they've got problems, but while they're thinking about what to do I'm killing them. Their minds are in the way, they can't survive me. We're over-running them.*

I have no remorse, killing people feels good. There was a woman, I had sex first before I killed her. It was her fault because she didn't enjoy it. We're having a party, we all feel really good. Now we're living in the big buildings. We've killed all the people. It's freezing.

But I'm looking around thinking, 'I couldn't build a building like this, or make these sweet-smelling gardens.' This place makes me feel not so animal — it lifts me up. It's all organised, it's not a forest, which is all I know.

Ah ... ah ... I feel so guilty! I know what I've done. They had as much right to live as I did. I feel really bad. It's hurting me physically in the heart, my emotions hurt me. I'm a bastard. I commit suicide. I put my sword up my rib cage and jump off a tall building.

It's hard to leave my body, I'm tied to it, I'm not completely dead. Ah, another realisation — my victims might have suffered for days.

As this fifth-century Goth warrior finally dies in a pool of blood, his killing lust extinguished by massive guilt, the time traveller's body feels intense pain that continues even after Azgar's death. Azgar's spirit does not want to leave the newly discovered gardens : 'I can't smell them now but I see them.' The spirit reports that a being in white tries to counsel him.

Being   *It's OK, it's like a flash in your existence, just a lesson, let go of the pain.*
Azgar   *How do you know?*
Being   *I've done it too. I've come to give you my thoughts.*

The barbarian's spirit begins to move up into higher consciousness, dragging his guilt. We find a way for him to drop some of the weight. Barry says, 'I feel different! My consciousness is expanding! I'm becoming everything!'

His journey into realms of higher awareness accelerates. Although his eyes are closed, his expression is full of awe as he identifies with a sacred state of being. When the inner event comes to its natural completion, identification drops away. He returns his focus to the room, dazed, realising he has just given himself an experience beyond price.

He also feels that he was born this time under a surgeon's blade because he killed not only others but himself too with a sword.

And by exploring a source of guilt, he has begun to dissipate his own entrenched guilt habit.

Guilt as a step to cosmic consciousness? Why not? Every feeling we have is a tool for learning and growing. As we clear our personal channel of energy blockages, layer by layer, we safely open our path to powerful transpersonal experiences.

Dr Stanislav Grof, a psychiatrist himself, describes such experiences as having extraordinary therapeutic potential of a quality exceeding much of psychiatry's offerings, through mechanisms beyond words. He comments on the irony of the fact that such phenomena are generally seen by psychiatry as pathological, and are suppressed.

However, psychiatry would agree that guilt is one of our heaviest burdens. It can ruin health and joy, part lovers and families, lay us open to political and religious manipulation, make Earth existence a misery, end lives. When we are stuck in guilt we inhibit our feelings, thoughts, behaviour and choices. These create our reality. Guilt blocks our inner progress, and it puts up barricades between us and other people.

Guilt, according to rebirthing writer Bob Mandel, is our mental Mafia.

Barry's emotional half-hour journey into what seems like the sack of Rome in AD 480 explored some of the unseen forces shaping his present life. Although this traveller had to wait 1500 years to recognise that episode in his soul history, he finally started to free up its bound energies.

GUILT, BLAME AND ANGER

Imagine a coin, one side marked 'guilt'. Flip it over, and there we find 'blame'. Guilt and blame fuse. When we dig deeply enough into one, we find the other. And blame is so often self-righteous anger. Guilt can have its roots in anger we may not know we have.

Sadly, an attitude of guilt is often more acceptable to ourselves and to others than if we were to acknowledge and safely express our deeply held rage — even though this could lead to dissolving both rage and guilt.

One of the many uses of past-life work is to tap into, and release, repressed or suppressed feelings. A story becomes a prism through which you view yourself. You may well feel safer contacting rage at, say, a long-dead gaoler who threatens your freedom in another life, than contacting rage at a present parent or spouse who has opposed you. Consciously, you may know nothing about the gaoler until he appears out of the mists of memory, but suddenly, amazingly, you are suffused with anger so great that you feel a blind urge to attack him. In the story you may even kill him.

Wherever has this emotion sprung from? Well, there's nobody there now but you...

Astonished as we get at this wealth of hidden feeling, we cannot be harbouring such an arsenal of secret energy without it having affected our behaviour in some way.

You might now recall a puzzling overreaction, such as when a gentle restraining hand on your arm triggered in you a surge of anger. You were not reacting to the moment, but to all the other times your liberty had been threatened or taken away. Your reaction showed you had not yet faced and dealt with those issues in the open, possibly because you felt guilty about wanting your own way.

A STORY OF SHAME
A past-life story that helped pour light into such a hidden vortex of guilt, shame and anger is set in Europe in the eighteenth century. Johannes, young son of a poor family, desperately wants to learn music. His parents give him as an apprentice to a domineering violinmaker. Living at the man's house, the boy discovers that the price of his apprenticeship is imprisonment and sexual slavery.

Totally cowed, abused for many years, sick and lonely, Johannes is convinced that he is rubbish, worthless. He grows to adulthood dedicated to his only comfort and inspiration, his talent for playing and creating violins. 'When I play,' he says, 'the notes go up to God.'

Even after his master's death, he is too ashamed to seek other company. Hearing the performance of a rising young violinist, he is struck down by jealousy. All that he had was his ability to make beautiful music, but here is talent so great that 'I would die for it,' Johannes says. When asked to make a violin for the boy he does so, but creates it slightly flawed. The flaw is noticeable only to him, but it is enough to dim slightly the splendour of the boy's playing.

Johannes falls into further guilt. Years later the boy he was jealous of has not been recognised, because of the violin. Johannes is steeped in chronic depression, in feelings of worthlessness, hate, bitterness and shame. When he becomes crippled with arthritis, he feels God is punishing him so that he cannot follow his calling. He dies in terror that God will not accept him.

The woman who painfully recalled this existence grew up in a respectable middle-class family, married happily and had children whom she and her husband nurtured. Yet all her life she had carried a deep sense of shame and guilt that apparently had no foundation. Discovering, and letting go of, the stress she unconsciously held from the violinmaker's life has supported her growing sense of self-worth. It was an important voluntary step on her spiritual path, her systematic exploration of unknown depths of her psyche, even though it meant that she had to face some unpleasant memories and experience temporary distress.

People who do not understand the steps of personal growth may mistake a healing crisis of this sort for something dangerous. Within the alternative therapies field, sometimes conditions seem to worsen before they get better. In fact, what is already there is simply being uncovered and owned so that it can be let go. Personal growth teachers liken this process to mud being stirred from a river bed to be washed away by the currents until the water runs clear.

Feeling our feelings does not mean we need to be stuck in them. If one of our feelings is that of being stuck, it is time to find a book or a tape telling us how to work through such a situation, or to go for help, which might be as simple as having a breathwork session.

We are all working through various challenges, knowingly or not. Probably most adults have mindlessly carried on some guilt from childhood in this life. Our weight of guilt may be additionally loaded from other lifetimes. And it has the habit of attracting repressive people into our lives, until we work through it.

A man struggled guiltily for months through a marriage breakup, believing what his wife kept telling him, that it was all his fault because he had not lived up to her material expectations. When he suddenly recognised that both people are responsible for their relationship, he was thunderstruck, and dropped the guilt in favour of allowing her equal responsibility.

Guilt accepted from relatives can distort lives. A young woman came to me in crisis, overwhelmed by hating her job as a child carer. She sobbed, 'But I can't leave it or I'll be letting my Dad down again.' Compounding her guilt was the fact that when her mother had died from cancer ten years previously, her distraught grandmother had said to her, 'You caused this, by not doing what she wanted.'

The story of a gentle young English girl, raped in a maze, seemed initially to have nothing to do with the present job crisis, although it surfaced spontaneously in Trudy's first rebirthing session that day. But later she left with hope and new resolve, all tears forgotten.

The past self had been engaged to a boy she'd known all her life. After the rape he rejected her as 'spoiled'. The rapist appeared as the new fiance of her widowed mother, and threatened the girl to silence. The rapist and the girl's fiance conspired to inject her with drugs that made her sicken and die painfully. The girl's fiance immediately married another local girl.

The key to the solution for Trudy's present dilemma was that the past self had instinctively felt there was 'something not right' about the engagement, but went into it anyway to please her mother. That decision led her to be murdered. Not only did Trudy see for herself the folly of adults pleasing parents to their own disadvantage, but also she discovered that the past self's mother was her present-day father, whom she was again trying to please by staying in a job she hated. To nurture herself, she left the job.

We can make guilt a way of life, an oh-so-subtle habit. Guilt addiction is established early in life and reinforced by parenting, by social, and possibly religious, pressures oriented to blame.

If you often or constantly feel guilty, there will be reasons for this. If the reason is that you are violating other people, it seems that sooner or later superjustice — karma — will catch you. But if you are simply accustomed to feeling guilty, you can recognise it as an old pattern you could drop. Perhaps you've done nothing to change your tendency to guilt because you don't recognise you have it. Or perhaps, although it's uncomfortable, it is at least familiar, and you fear change.

ROOTS OF GUILT

The roots of guilt, in fact, may be so deep in this lifetime that they reach back to birth. As Dr Verny describes, in both womb and birth canal the foetus is an aware, feeling being, capable of receiving gut-level impressions. Rebirthing experiences show that if a mother suffers greatly in childbirth, the foetus can imprint with guilt for hurting her.

Whatever we 'say' to ourselves, or decide, in time of trauma, goes deep into the subconscious and becomes an order we follow afterwards. It feels like truth. People are discovering that this applies even to infants, before they have words or conscious thought. Even stages of a normal birth are felt by the baby to be traumatic and life-threatening — not unreasonably, as vast numbers of children have died in the birth canal. Large numbers of people recall feeling guilty during birth trauma. But as a baby moves on safely into life, his or her unconscious, emotional logic then becomes, 'When I feel guilty, I survive.' This locking in of primal guilt with the survival instinct sets up a largely unrecognised negative pattern called by rebirthers the Infant Guilt Syndrome. It predisposes people to later habits of guilt, reinforced through disapproval from others.

Babies may identify with their mother's thoughts that the baby is responsible for their pain. (Some mothers who have not released their own trauma around giving birth remind a child even into adulthood, 'You gave me 20 hours of hell!', or 'You were our big mistake!', even 'You ripped my insides out!') However, modern teachers of ideal birthing methods claim that in the absence of physical abnormality, responsibility generally lies, not with the presence of the baby, but with a number of other factors that affect the mother's own attitudes and rigidify her body. These include residual tensions and conscious or unconscious fears from her own uncleared birth trauma, which prevent her body and mind from embracing a natural experience as some women are able to do.

Babies who do not imprint with guilt at birth may not have brought in guilt issues from previous lives, or may have felt so secure throughout life in the womb that guilt did not arise during birth.

Once the Infant Guilt Syndrome is established in the nervous system, people unknowingly play it out in varying degrees of intensity. They may silently and stubbornly resist taking steps to more fulfilment in life because of unrecognised guilt ('I don't deserve better'). Or they may be so upfront with guilt that they apologise not only for their own actions, feelings and thoughts, but also for other people's, the weather, and anything else they can find. Some people are even smug about how guilty they feel ('so I must be a good person!').

Others think they want to let guilt go, yet unknowingly resist. During a wet rebirthing session in a hot tub — where the breather hangs underwater, breathing through a snorkel to simulate hanging in the amniotic fluid of the womb — a man who habitually suffered a lot of physical pain relived his prenatal months. He realised his mother felt extremely guilty about circumstances in her life. As a foetus he was not aware of being a separate being. Physically he and his mother were one, and emotionally he was ultra-responsive to her. He felt that her guilt became his guilt.

However, when he surfaced and told me this and I asked, 'Do you want to let the guilt go now?' his instant response was a resounding 'No!' This shocked him deeply. It caused him to look at whether he was unwilling to give up guilt because he himself used it as a weapon on others. In many households parents rule the family through guilt, and those children become adults who repeat the process.

We also discussed whether guilt feelings might be connected with his physical pain, as they often seem to be. Guilt invites punishment. He felt hopeful that this line of exploration might reduce his pain.

JUDGEMENT MUST BE RELATIVE

Events that make people in our culture feel guilty may have been regarded differently in other cultures. In past lifetimes exploration, naturally we are tempted to take our present values back, to judge people of the past by the mores of our own society. But this is not always valid.

One issue that tempts judgement is prostitution. History shows that throughout the centuries in patriarchal societies around the globe, before social welfare payments, countless women often saw no way to survive but by selling their only asset, their body.

A middle-aged widow discovers for herself that in a past life two centuries ago she became a prostitute, to get money for food and shelter. She is shocked and ashamed. Even though she admits, 'Well, that certainly explains how I feel about men now', she feels grief and guilt for several days. She now has a choice. She can do the further work necessary to begin to change her self-fulfilling and quite justified belief, according to her past experience, that she can't trust men to be kind or to respect her. Or she can allow the programming she has been unconscious of to continue either attracting the kind of men she doesn't want, or keeping her away from kinder partners.

Prostitution has been regarded in various ways throughout the ages. The following story comes from a Mediterranean country in a time so ancient that its customs and values are alien to ours. Yet emotions bridge the gap.

THE STORY OF A TEMPLE PROSTITUTE

This is the story of Alostra, a temple prostitute, whose parenthood is mysterious and taps into legend. According to the records of a number of ancient societies, at one time tall blond 'giants' travelled through countries, mating with local peasant women, apparently to seed new racial strains. Beautiful blond children commonly resulted and, in Alostra's country, the custom was that such children were given to temples at an early age to perform sacred service to the gods. As the story unfolds, a sinister aspect of this temple stewardship emerges.

This example illustrates the interface of past lifetime, past death and present birth that transpersonal counsellors have been discovering in recent decades.

Recall of Alostra was preceded by recall of June's birth 40 years before. June's mother had eloped against her parents' wishes. Two years after the marriage, her husband left her soon after June's conception, which June feels took place in marital violence. Without money and shattered by both breakup and pregnancy, June's mother felt she had to go home to her newly widowed mother, a situation of bitterness for both women.

Re-experiencing the incredible sensitivity of the newborn, June realised that judgemental obstetric staff suspected this unwanted baby was illegitimate. She absorbed the delivery team's attitudes of blame and censure, probably an echo of her mother's home situation throughout the pregnancy. So June was primed to feel worthless and ashamed even before she had left her mother's body. She did not want to come out into such a threatening world.

June also took on guilt from the 36-hour gruelling labour that she and her reluctant mother went through. Re-experiencing her mother wanting to expel her 'like a piece of shit', she began to see where her own feelings of guilt for existing had begun. As an adult, June is able to put words to memories of sensations and gut reactions she recalled experiencing as a baby.

Regression: (Present-life birth) *Stainless steel, antiseptic smell, my head is spinning, a clamp at my forehead. No, I don't want to. Big people, arms and hair, I feel sick. She's gone, full of anaesthetic. I'm still in her, my belly is being squeezed in her. I want to say, 'You're a slut, a slut', I can't get the message out. I'm the same as her, I'm a slut, I'm no good, I know I'm a whore.*

(Past-life: voice changes to a light patter.) What women are for is to serve the man. My purpose is fulfilment from serving the man. Whatever he wants, it's good for me. I'm an adult female, very beautiful, delicate, lovely skin, blonde. Alostra. My beauty is a divine purpose, a gift for all the men, their pleasure is my delight, I love to serve. Men give me delight, allow me to serve with my body.

I learned this at the Temple School, a place of elegance, beauty, pleasure, and the teaching. Our country is Estra, a very noble country. I am noble, very pure, and I delight to serve.

My mother was a peasant, little and dark, someone I passed through to go to the School, a vessel. My father was a blond man, very big, passing through. He gave his seed to my mother for me to be born and go to the School.

I learn the male pleasure. I serve the spiritually elite, they respect my skills. It's a holy service because their pleasure is my delight. I have many pleasuring ways. I'm a gift from the gods.

Some men dream when they take their pleasure, they release from Earth to the stars. Not that one! He's cunning, tries to hurt me, pinches my tender parts. He's slippery, sly, peers around corners. He's jealous, wants to interfere, break the spell, the beauty. He comes from across the sea, he wants power.

Oh, no-one believes me, that he wants to hurt me. He tells them he's like them and they let him be with me. I'm at the palace. He's vile, vile, disturbing the flow. He's not divine, he brings in base wishes.

I want to protect myself, they won't believe me. He spoils my beauty, says I'm a whore, a base creature. He's of another faith. He's Calistra. He thinks I'm evil. The others know the truth, I'm in divine service.

He limps, drags his foot around the palace, he hoodwinks them, visiting to spy. He makes me feel terrible, he's so ugly I feel defiled. The light is going. I lived in a beautiful light of service and delight, he's poisoning that. I feel bad. I hate him, he says things to me, whisper, whisper, says I'm bad. Why does he come and spread his filth? I've never hated anyone.

He's going home in a month. They can't see what he's doing. I was a child of the gods, he has defiled me. My graceful day has gone. I had to be there for him, an honoured visitor. Oh, the ship has come, I can live again. I belong to the Temple, and I will purify.

Oh God, he has impregnated me. I don't want it, the child, never, never. I will abort, the sacred herbs. Oh, oh, they say I must have the child, courtesy, diplomatic relations. They will not herb me! I don't want to live.

Where is my golden day? He is gone, laughing, laughing. I cannot leave. The flame of hating, calling itself a child. I will not have this emissary's brat, I would rather kill myself. There must be another way, they will not herb me. I'm in torment, every moment of this pregnancy is torment, he never ceases to laugh, I know he laughs. No way out but sacred herbs or kill myself. I'm not brave enough to lance the baby's head.

I'll never go back to my golden days, he's killed them, there's another in my place. My feelings don't matter. They give me the treatment, I lose myself in the depths of the sacred flame. 'It's an honour, I'm specially chosen to have this child, I love and protect this child.' My head says no. 'I honour this child from afar.'

I sit void in the garden. A letter from him to my teachers, 'Safeguard the mother, she must be untouched by other men.' Time for the sacred flame. 'I love this child, honour and serve this new man-child whose pleasure is my delight.' He plays in the sand and I help him, he crows and coos, his pleasure is my delight. Why is my heart heavy? I do my job well.

Now he's grown and they take him from me, to his father.

I wither and die. He is a gift for his father. The child too has known the sacred flame, 'an honour to serve'. I wither and die, slowly shrinking, used up, wrinkling and shrinking, scratching the earth. Goat meat, they send it.

I have dreams of the golden time, it doesn't last, they take it away. Emptiness and death. Don't sap me of my life, don't dry me up! Sunburned, on the sand, dying, a husk, a shell, empty inside. Ants crawl in my mouth. My mouth is a silent cry, all is lost. My body was so beautiful that men would queue to serve me. Hyenas tear my body. I'm not there.

After dying stamped with the shame of rejection and ugliness, Alostra/June is conceived in violence perhaps 3000 years later, to a mother who probably yearned to abort her as Alostra had wanted to abort 'the emissary's brat'. June is born into a rejecting family, with forceps distorting her head so that she is temporarily ugly.

One of the many things this story illuminated for June was her previous revulsion for the practice of hypnosis. The sacred flame used as a hypnotic control tool by temple authorities still burned brightly enough in her psyche for her to be born this time into a religion that denounces hypnosis.

In the 20th century, as she clears the issues of then and now, she hopes to complete a cycle arching through linear time, so that the rest of this life can be free of the constricting feelings and beliefs she'd gathered, especially guilt about sexuality. As a bonus, she hopes that she will not need to repeat such misery in future lives!

AN INNER STORY

We may perceive a story within June's story. Initial time in the womb, the first part of a pregnancy, is called by obstetrician Dr Frederick Leboyer 'the golden age' in his classic book *Birth Without Violence*. ('I'll never go back to my golden days,' cries Alostra in anguish.) Dr Leboyer describes the early time of establishment and growth we each experienced within the sheltering womb as a time of limitless contentment and freedom.

He likens the normal embryo to a small plant, growing and blossoming into a foetus, enjoying gentle movements while buoyed up in fluid, 'weightless, light as a bird, agile and lively as a fish'. The foetus continues to grow but the womb eventually stops expanding. When the little body fills available space to the point of imprisonment, the pressures of the birth journey or the surgeon's intervention end womb life — so that something greater can occur.

Within her mother's body June experienced both her 'golden days' and the Infant Guilt Syndrome. The dynamics of these foetal elements appear in her story of the temple prostitute.

June carried Alostra's issues of guilt and worthlessness into her own life. While she was still a baby, her mother passed over June's upbringing into the hands of her mother. The grandmother was an uneducated woman who loved her but

101

who behaved like a martyr, reinforcing June's guilt every day. And with a total absence of June's father, and a taboo on all questions about him, June as a child decided that somehow it must also be her fault that he was absent.

She had developed what is now called, in personal growth terms, a shame-based personality.

In working to clear these enormous issues, she finally reached a state of forgiveness for herself, her parents and her grandmother. The constant grinding stresses she had previously lived under dropped away as her life circumstances began to improve.

PAST AND PRESENT GUILTS

There is no shortage of hooks on which to hang guilt feelings. Some reasons people find for feeling guilty are understandable, others seem absurd to observers not themselves enmeshed in this pattern.

Present life reasons for feeling guilty that people have shared with me include: simply existing at all; being illegitimate, unwanted, adopted or unloved; being a failure, or being successful; being poor or having money; being stupid, a disappointment, ill or alcoholic; being suspicious of parents or disliking in-laws; not keeping promises; feeling pleasure, withholding in intimate relationships, or breaking the boys-don't-cry taboo; being the first twin to emerge, or an only survivor of twins; having an abortion, having one's child drown or having a child's birth advanced; being a 'bad' parent or child; needing a parent to go to work to feed and clothe oneself as a child; leaving the family; 'depressing my husband through my troubles'; being absent when a pet died; an acquaintance's suicide, the death of a grandparent or sibling; a mother's illnesses, miscarriage, suicide or death in childbirth; the death of a spouse from cancer; having sex with a stranger, a lover, or even a husband; being sexually attacked, being forced into incest.

Guilt issues brought from past lifetimes echo all these 'reasons', and add historical colour. Each culture makes its own laws, and consequently its own guilts. A crime in one society is revered in another, as when, for example, a past self reveals that murder is seen as a sacred sacrifice to save a nation from famine.

A monk feels guilty for failing to heal people during the black plague; an Aboriginal man for not attempting single-handed rescue of his tribe from an attacking tribe; a Turk for killing a Christian ('What will his God do to me?'); a general for sending others to their deaths for his own ambition; a man for rebelling to achieve his own needs; a respectable merchant for keeping a mistress; a thief for stealing to eat; a serf for not being able to protect his family from massacre by feudal landowners killing for sport; a mediaeval squire for choosing marriage instead of 'a spiritual task'; a politician for starting a war for revenge; a sailor for falling off a ship and being too weak to save himself from drowning; a Napoleonic soldier for desertion; a Chinese woman for binding the feet of girl children; a soldier for shooting children; a widow for committing suicide; a cleric for sexual indiscretions; a woman for 'being only human' although her contemporaries had set her up as a goddess figure.

An American writer (a woman's past self) relieved himself of a guilty secret after his death. He told his present self — and his regression guide — that 40 years before he died he had committed an unrecognised murder.

A sterile man believes the condition arises out of his guilt in a past life, when, as another man desperate for sons, he sent away a barren wife, and two of his subsequent wives died in childbirth.

A woman is shocked to find that one of her past selves was a criminal. The news precipitates her into a healing crisis. For some days she feels overwhelmed by guilt and shame. Then she asks for help. In session, we briefly explore guilt and shame in her own life.

Then we go into the other life, clarify exactly what happened, what forces were acting on the past self to create the situation, and what the feelings were. This involves both the woman and the past character in self-examination and reflection. By the end of the consultation, the woman understands more about herself, feels at peace, and has accessed new hope for a present problem that had seemed insurmountable. She has forgiven the past self. Farewelling that self with thanks for the illumination, she says excitedly, 'She even looks as though she feels forgiven!'

Psychic weights hiding in the present-day guilt patterns of

individuals have emerged as past lifetime acts such as kidnapping, manslaughter, torture and failure. Some travellers dimly suspected that something dreadful had happened to them in a past life, or that they had done something dreadful. Dropping such burdens means letting fresh air into the past. But being willing to move through the stages of forgiveness and release can take courage.

One avenue of help is the following process, which demands great honesty.

The process is oriented only to peace-making within oneself, not to any outcome with others. To benefit, people who feel guilty need to look deep enough into themselves to discover their blaming habit. For example, if you feel guilty for existing, probably deep down you blame your parents for conceiving you. Blame may be reasonable and accurate, yet staying stuck in it will hurt only the blamer.

A FORGIVENESS PROCESS
to release guilt and blame

This process can be done about people having an impact on your present life, even if they have died. It may also be done as, or with, past lifetime characters.

* Working alone, or with a guide, lie down, close your eyes and use your favourite relaxation process and/or soft music to reach a state of deep relaxation.
* Acknowledge aloud your intention to heal a specific state of non-forgiveness, of another person, or of yourself
* Acknowledge your true feelings about the situation: the resentment, anger or hate you have been holding against someone else, or the shame, disgust or anger against yourself. Allow yourself to feel these feelings fully. Breathe deeply.

TO RELEASE GUILT
1. Visualise the person you feel you have wronged.
2. Talk aloud to this person about the situation, from your heart. Say everything you need to say. Explain exactly how the situation happened, how you felt and feel.
3. You may like to ask this person's forgiveness. If so, be open to receiving an impression of an answer rather than imagining one.

---

4. More importantly, as you can't choose for anyone else, can you yet forgive yourself? If not, keep talking until at least you understand how you cam to behave in that way. Explain how you would prefer to handle a similar situation in the future.

TO RELEASE BLAME
1. Visualise a cardboard or stuffed 'copy' of the person you can't forgive.
2. To honour your anger, spend time mentally acting out with the copy, exactly what you would like to do to punish that person, no holds barred. Do this as a child might fantasise revenge, until it is all out of your system. To intensify, you might act out this punishment physically by bashing a mattress, twisting a towel and/or yelling.
3. Then mentally ask the person you are visualising (not the copy) to explain his or her point of view and feelings about the situation you had not forgiven. Do not put words into his or her mouth. Listen inwardly, that is, take your first impressions of the response.

Keep 'discussing' the situation, until you feel a measure of understanding, completion or peace.

* Now examine your feelings. Has there been a shift? If not, you have not contacted nor expressed the depth of your feelings. Repeat the process.
* To express the new state of your relationship, visualise or feel yourself making some physical gesture with the other person, a handshake or a hug. Perhaps you are starting to feel love that has been below the pain all along.
* Realise that your heart is now open, forgiveness is your truth, and you are free. Acknowledge yourself for healing this old pain. Celebrate!

(With both guilt and blame, some violations are so massive that forgiveness seems not only impossible but even undesirable. Then the opportunity is to move to a deeper level of experiential inner work, to heal effects on yourself, and so demonstrate hope for others.)

Chapter Seven

Illness and Pain

Lee has recently started herbal studies but has difficulty remembering the names of herbs. She has also begun to suffer severe migraines.

Regression: I'm in a chapel, I have taken the veil. I wear a white dress with a cord, black shoes, my hair tucked in. My face is round with red cheeks. My peasant parents sent me to live with the nuns when I was five, because we were poor. I felt sad and lost when my brother drove me there in a cart. But now I feel tears of happiness.

I used to wear dark clothes. At 15 I ran around the fields with other girls, picking flowers and berries. I see the grey stone walls of the convent, the land is flat and green.

Now I've taken the veil I'm more responsible, I can't run around. I work in the garden. God is there. I love God. My name is Mary. I can't see how the veil looks, there are no mirrors in the convent, mirrors are for people who are idle and vain. I pray to help the sisters in the infirmary, to work with the one who makes medicines from plants. They won't let me, they say I'm not clever enough. (She cries.)

One of the sisters says I can help her, I'm happy. We dig herbs and make lotions. Now it's autumn. I'm gathering hawthorn berries, you get scratched hands but it's worth it. There's a raggedy boy who wants to know about the plants.

I'm thinking of going up the convent tower. You're alone there, a good view. I'm not happy. I don't seem to get on with things. There's trouble. In the distillery something has gone off, it looks a bit different. Oh, it's made someone very ill. People blame me, I should have tipped it out. But then they'd have been cross with me. I should go to confession. No, I'll just pray.

Another time I see those red berries, maybe they got mixed up too and went into the wrong medicine. {She cries.} *It's dark here in the distillery.*

Maybe I should kill myself, everything goes wrong, the nuns blame me. Dear God, dear God, it's the bishop. He's still alive. No, now he's died.

I'm not allowed in the distillery any more, they think it was my fault.

I'm older now. I notice I can feel things with my hands, whether people have pain or not, or if it's good medicine or not. It feels like pins and needles. When it's not good, my hands stay cold. I can help some of my sisters, when they have a headache I put my hands on them and it goes away.

I had to go to Mother Superior. They think it's the work of the Devil. She's not sure though. Other nuns say, 'If it's not, who is she — a stupid girl who gets things mixed up — to do the work of Jesus, if we can't do that?' I'm forbidden to do it. I'm sad. But I hate myself for not doing it. The power comes from God. I am disobeying God.

I'm 30 now. Mother Superior is saying, 'You killed the bishop, now you want to indoctrinate the sisters in the work of the Devil!' She's warned me before. Now I'm not even allowed to be with the others, I have to stay in my cell, it's dark and damp. I've been weeks and weeks alone. I have to stay here till I die. I pray and cry. Sometimes I see a little bird who has a nest nearby. Sometimes I see the sun a bit. I might as well die now as later.

When Clare brings food I ask her to leave my door unlocked so I can have a breath of fresh air. She's let me out before, nobody knew. I pray for her not to feel guilty. I go up the tower. I look out at the countryside. I'm sad I couldn't make a better job of everything. (I can't leave the convent, no, I've never even thought of it, nobody would have me.) This will be a deadly sin and I'm going straight to hell. I pray, but what's the use if I'm going to hell? I jump. I just close my eyes and take a step forward. I hit my head on the stone. There's a big pain in my head, blood oozing out. My back hurts. Dull pains, throbbing head.

Is that all?

I see the raggedy boy. But how can I, when my face is down? He gets a fright when he sees all the blood, runs away. It's evening now.

So I jumped after all. I can't understand why I'm not in hell. I just look at this figure down there. I feel sorry for poor little Mary, I must have died. I feel angry that I was cheated, that all the nuns who had power over me cheated me of my gift of healing.

107

Lee and I work with this story in consecutive sessions, exploring the emotions, releasing the physical trauma, and looking at Mary's negative belief systems. We find Lee has brought into this life traces of feeling 'I'm stupid' and 'I'm dangerous', which stress her as she again tries to be a herbalist. It's as though her mind fogs up because some deep part of her does not want her to succeed — because working with herbs once led her to kill another, and herself.

We also deal briefly with two more of Lee's past selves. One is a lonely schoolteacher who feels he is trapped in the monotony of English village life. He too suffers intermittent head pain and nausea, and finally dies from them.

The second is a teenage Hindu fisherman, forced to marry a rich, nagging old woman for the dowry she brings to his poor family. Goaded into rage, he shakes her while his brother tries to stop him by hitting his head with an oar. They find he has strangled her. Later, remorseful, he slips while pulling in a net and falls overboard, fatally striking his head on the boat.

After the sessions, Lee's study difficulties with confusion ease. She has since become a successful qualified herbalist. And after the sessions, her migraines immediately diminished.

What caused the physical improvement?

These three stories that had hidden in Lee's subconscious all involved damage centering around the head. We had investigated the nun's story because it had seemed to Lee to be the most urgent of the three. We discussed the idea that perhaps each damage incident represented a layer of stress still held in her consciousness. In some mysterious way, these had coalesced into physical manifestation as the present self's agonising migraines.

Although there is no guarantee of health improvement following past-life work, many international practitioners report improvement for clients in some physical problems. Past-life work does not treat disease, yet it can mysteriously and dramatically relive deep-seated stress, which may allow body systems to revitalise themselves.

Excessive stress has been shown to cause oxygen deficiency in body cells. Oxygen deficiency is claimed as the single greatest physical cause of both disease and body deterioration with age.

A STOMACH ULCER

Linda is a young working mother who took part in a private research study of mine. This was a different kind of oral history study, in which volunteers visited a particular stage of their past-life history under hypnosis. Linda did not believe in reincarnation but was intrigued by the novelty of exploring her consciousness. Later, she told me that frequent digestive problems, with irritability and depression, had plagued her since she was at high school. Seven years before, a stomach ulcer had been diagnosed.

We began to explore experiences that seemed to be of past lives. She felt she was a knight, lanced in the stomach in a jousting contest. He fell off his horse and died. We noted that the area of fatal damage was the stomach.

Next, Linda reported feeling as though she were a child crawling on a railway line. She found this hard to believe but the image persisted. Along came a train and cut the infant in two, severing the body at the stomach.

Linda's first reaction was horror. Courageously, she agreed to work through it. She was able to recall the death scene several times until the emotional charge had left it. Then she became aware of a woman in long skirts and other children finding the baby's body. Linda, a mother herself, felt extremely angry: 'How could any mother let a child crawl on a railway line?' I encouraged her to feel deep into the anger. After she had expressed it by telling off her past-life mother, the anger faded away.

The following week, Linda said on the phone that she had started to feel better the day after the session. She had just been to hospital for a laparoscopy. No ulcer was found. Throughout the following year she managed a heavy workload far more easily than before.

FALL FROM A HORSE

Mandy is a remedial masseuse who for years had been hampered by pain in her right shoulder. We uncovered a lifetime in which she was crippled on her right side because of an accident while riding a horse wildly in a rage, feeling misunderstood by everyone around her. We healed the lifetime in the sense that she relived it powerfully, confronted its joys and pressures, and finished its old emotional business.

Just before the accident the woman in the life story had ached to hit out physically (with her right arm) at a suitor who did not appreciate her needs. Mandy smiled with satisfaction as she experienced her past self battering an imagined copy of this man. Only then did she feel free to make a true peace with him.

Mandy felt she then contacted a spiritual guide energy, which 'laid hands' on her shoulder, and told her that her inner work had healed it although there would be slight soreness for three months. This proved to be what happened — after her next step.

The continuing vibrations of this centuries-old story disturbed a stagnant relationship in Mandy's present family life. Anger that surfaced in her regression remained with her afterwards. Recognising it as her own, she used it to confront what she was unhappy about in the present. Now she was able to say to the person, 'I'm really angry about what's happening. Are you willing to work it through with me?' Changes for the better resulted from their exchange. Perhaps, subconsciously. her arm had been wanting to hit a particular family member, but she had not let herself realise this until she'd discovered and explored anger through the story.

The chronic pain diminished to nothing. Two years later the shoulder is still pain-free.

AUSCHWITZ MEMORY
Can we really bring illness into this life from other lifetimes?

Eve, a fifteen-year-old Australian girl, developed a severe rash on her right arm inside the elbow. No medical remedies made any difference, but finally it went away. Ten years later, Eve experienced a session of rebirthing, during which two spontaneous impressions came to her.

In the first scene, she briefly felt she was someone else, a 15-year-old girl on a train with soldiers; she felt a burning pain in her arm, and the word 'Auschwitz' came to her. In the second scene, the same girl — thin, with a shaven head — was forcibly held down while men branded her arm. The branding site on the European girl was the site of the rash which had appeared on the arm of the Australian girl, at the same age, 40 years later.

Eve was excited by this World War II memory flash. She said, 'I understood then that the rash was like old pain that I'd needed to let go.'

In session, a woman felt that she experienced dying, as a woman in a previous life, from the effects of a cancerous right ovary. The woman herself has a diseased right ovary. She says, 'I'd better get it seen to.'

THE MULTI-DIMENSIONAL SELF

American physician Dr Richard Gerber writes in his book *Vibrational Medicine* that energetics medicine views illness holistically, as a sign of blockage somewhere in the multi-dimensional self. He claims that illnesses express blocked emotional and spiritual states.

Holistic healing rejects the practice of considering physical symptoms in isolation and instead takes into account the whole person, at the energetic levels of body, mind, emotions and — as through past lifetimes counselling — spirit.

Since the first medical body/mind clinic opened in the US in 1969, linkings of mind, emotions and body have come to be widely accepted as factors in health. Even orthodox medical literature discusses emotional effects on health. People are generally becoming more aware that their inner states create either health or illness.

Look around your community and notice, for example, all the people whose bodies are bent and broken. Could these distortions stem from mental and emotional pain trapped below conscious awarenesss, out of their own lives and/or their past lives? Could this mean that as we learn to do our self-transformation work — to complete with our past — we no longer need regard such conditions as unavoidable?

EMOTIONAL PAIN IGNORED

Psychologist Erich Fromm has said that while most car owners notice and attend to strange noises or knocks in their cars, they don't do the same for themselves. Many of us do not deal with our emotional pain because we are not aware of how to do it, nor of how such issues can affect our health and life situations.

An older man in an advanced stage of cancer, son of undemonstrative parents from England says, 'I've always detested displays of affection.'

A woman told me, 'I'm such a happy person, I've got everything. A lovely home, a loving husband, although he's had a stroke. I walk on the beach and feel close to God. My mother brought me up to try never to be angry. Of course, I did get cancer, so I suppose I had some stress.'

Medical studies show correlations between the repression of anger and the development of some cancers and other major diseases. A study of past, as well as present, lifetimes of people with such conditions may well show similar patterns of emotional holding-in. However, their soul histories may also contain lifetimes where they were freely in touch with their emotions, a capacity worth reviving in their present circumstances.

'Don't cry!' comes from people whose own tears are locked inside. But the energy of denied emotions must eventually go somewhere. A psychotherapist said, 'My grandmother's house was peaceful, but violent people came out of it.' Violence, the result of repressing anger until it explodes, can be expressed against others or against ourselves. Most of us have to discover ways to safely express anger. As knowledge increases of the effects of not allowing emotions to flow easily, much illness begins to seem like unconscious self-violation.

In past lifetime terms, perhaps rebirth is a case of 'Once more, with feeling!' Must we reincarnate on Earth's stage again and again, to learn to accept all our emotions, all parts of ourselves, however undeveloped? The good news is that we have a choice: to remain emotionally crippled, if that's how we seem to be, or to love ourselves so much that we commit to healing our numbness.

The woman of 50 whose mother taught her 'to try never to be angry' is choosing to obey an instruction 45 years out of date, rather than to become responsible for herself in the present. The instruction was the best her mother knew at the time. Yet, with today's knowledge, it seems to be lethal advice.

MULTIPLE PERSONALITY DISORDER

People who still doubt the links between disease and states of consciousness need only look to new studies of individuals suffering from Multiple Personality Disorder. Hearing inner voices that won't go away does not always mean schizophrenia, say specialists in this controversial syndrome. Movies such as *The Three Faces of Eve* and *Sybil* (who showed evidence of twenty-eight subpersonalities) have been followed by books from former sufferers whose personalities integrated through treatment, or who learned to live harmoniously in MPD mode.

Most different personalities shown by an individual with MPD may not be aware of others. Each may have different health problems, allergic reactions, responses to drugs, cardio-vascular function, menstrual cycles, immunological response, brainwave and voice patterns, as well as handwriting, intelligence levels and taste in clothes. Even scars, burn marks and cysts can vary with each personality. Identities can interchange rapidly. One personality of an individual can be drunk, another suddenly comes in sober. A person admitted to hospital suffering from diabetes can instantly test clear when another personality takes over. At least one blind MPD sufferer can see, when other personalities emerge. Some people need to carry several pairs of glasses in different prescriptions.

Personalities exhibited by an MPD sufferer may seem to be children or adults of either sex. A past lifetimes practitioner must wonder if any are connected with past incarnations. I speculate on whether the overriding 'I' of the sufferer calls on the core essence of personalities already within consciousness — past selves — to surface in a present environment, stripped of their historical context, and employed only in their bare essentials of outlook and attitude. The purpose could be to buffer the individual from the full impact of the original trauma believed to have created the condition.

If this were discovered to be so, those past selves may thus offer more healing options within a difficult therapeutic challenge. After all, past selves show themselves willing enough to come forward in consciousness in regression, with a variety of helpful results.

Science writer Michael Talbot comments that because both psyche and body of the MPD can switch from one biological state to another immediately, the unknown control systems that mastermind these changes are awe-inspiring.

With MPDs, each change of personality actually heals physical dysfunction in the body, even if temporarily, to a degree that responds, for example, to hospital testing for diabetes. The diabetes is locked into only one, or some, of the personalities expressing through the one body. This seems to illustrate that physical dysfunction is anchored in the personality — or individual consciousness — rather than in the body as we have always supposed. And, as instantaneous healing is possible for some human bodies, it's likely to be possible for all, given the necessary circumstances (which may not need to be MPD!).

This amazing revelation moves us into considering the realm of the new metaphysics, where consciousness is seen to affect physicality. This is the principle that thought, conscious or unconscious, creates results.

This is a foundational concept in subatomic physics, the study of the micro-world that underlies everyday appearances. Quantum science recognises that observers, by their presence alone as conscious beings, are likely to affect the results of experiments. In fact, even orthodox science requires double-blind approaches to experiments in case an experimenter's thoughts influence results.

Metaphysics has been called 'the science of ultimate causation'. Metaphysically, a serious ailment that has manifested in the physical body will probably be seen to have a number of ultimate, or metaphysical, causes. As Dr Gerber describes, this means it results from a chain of emotional, mental and/or spiritual blockages in consciousness. Not surprisingly, these blockages often involve uncleared trauma. Understanding why we have some problem is not enough to shift physical manifestations of stress, although it has a relieving effect mentally. We must also connect experientially with the blocked emotions.

Metaphysically, a physical problem may require each layer of old energy blockage to be dealt with, as in one particular case of narcolepsy (a severe sleep compulsion) where 14 emotional causes were revealed through body feedback testing. The client was not willing to stay the distance for experimental clearing! At other times I have experienced that working through only one or two deep-seated causes has allowed the body to release an ailment.

Metaphysical causes of a physical ailment can link present discomfort with birth, past lives and past deaths. A man suffering hip spasm and pain that often interfered with sleep said, 'This has haunted me all my life.' In a rebirthing session, he felt that at his birth a doctor was holding his malleable newborn body upside down by the feet, and that this was damaging his hip. Then, although his Christian upbringing discouraged him from believing in past lives, he reluctantly coped with intense and dramatic spontaneous impressions, ranging from a lion attack on the hip through to sensations of a severely crippled leg, to feeling he was an unpopular soldier who was roped by the leg and swung over a cliff by drunken fellow soldiers.

REGRESSION BODY RESPONSES
As in rebirthing, people in regression can experience many body responses. This is direct evidence of mind/body connections. Responses might be temporary pain, heat, cold, tingling, flushing, tightness, numbness and even cramping. Sites of old ailments or operations may experience rushes of energy. In one session, sudden pain in the neck and head followed a woman's discovery of a suicidal hanging by a past self, until we ran the memory quickly backwards and forwards to defuse it. Stories involving pressure on past selves' bodies can produce pressure on the traveller's body. Even more than imagery, such sensations impress travellers with the validity of these stories.

OBSERVING A SESSION
To illustrate, let's follow a breath therapy session with Maria, a design student who unaccountably dissolved into tears, confusion and severe anxiety when she won her first award for stained-glass artwork. As soon as she began to tell me about her success, she started crying. Tears throughout the session came first from fear and sadness, later from relief, love for her mother, then gratitude for her own deep love of beauty.

Maria's body is a faster monitor than many other people's, which makes her mind/body connections clear. She is basically healthy but has a few minor health problems. None are evident as we start the session. I explain to her how to use a quick-release breath technique. From a session lasting two hours, these are the main points.

We begin by examining Maria's fears of success, and soon arrive at a major belief she carries, which feels like truth to her: 'My success hurts others.' Her neck immediately feels tight. As more deep, self-defeating beliefs surface, her whole body tightens. She whispers, 'There are so many things I'm frightened of.'

The next belief we uncover is, 'If I'm beautiful, people will hate me.' This includes, 'If I create beauty, people will hate me.' Maria shivers, feels soreness in her neck, and a burning in her head and under her ribs. She uses her breath to release the

115

bodily discomfort. 'I hurt people' brings fresh tears. 'I love people and they don't understand' triggers such severe back pain that she cries out. Shifting, she says, 'Perhaps it's the way I'm sitting.' The pain persists.

Maria says, 'Oh, I feel like I've been whipped. I shouldn't be here. I'm making up someone's life. I'm in the way !' Her ears burn. 'I feel I've been dipped in hot water.' A sensation comes of something heavy across her shoulders. Is she experiencing the stirring of past-life stories linked with her present body, mind and feelings?

We move on through incidents in her childhood. 'I felt guilty for just about everything,' she sighs. 'I feel responsible for everyone around me. I love them so much.' She bursts into tears again. 'I've died because I've loved. I don't know where that thought came from.'

She yelps, from a stabbing pain above her left breast ('I've had this pain before'). Her stomach churns. When she calms, we continue, trusting the twists and turns of this path on which her breath is leading her, tracking to deep origins of her current problem.

While impressions of her mother stir tears of love, she says, 'If I'm truly myself I'll lose everyone's respect, love and help.' As we release this belief another comes up: 'Someone will steal my success and I'll starve.'

New images bring stabbing pains to her shoulders and neck. 'I feel as if I'm being cut,' she says. 'I see a warrior, Japanese, and a woman in white, kneeling. There's something wrong. A lot of metal around. Blood. Oh, it's something about caste, the woman is high caste, I'm not, I'm the warrior. But we love each other so much.' This brings more pain in her back, more tears.

'I'm just making this up,' says Maria. 'She's thrown into something. A blindfold, a rope. Then silence. I feel incredible pain in my chest, I want to die. Kill me! A man holds a sharp sword, he feels like my father, I love him too. He swings the sword — there's a head rolling. It looks a bit comical. The warrior was thinking, "What a waste, to end it this way, there's such a lot to learn."'

Maria takes a minute to recover from the shock of the beheading Her own chest pain subsides, but she rubs her shoulders and neck. 'I have such a lot of problems in my upper

116

back, I'm constantly going to the chiropractor.' We discuss how these physical problems may be rooted in physical and emotional trauma from her past, and magnified by her belief that she has to 'carry' other people She feels she carries the world on her shoulders.

Maria comments that the beheading seems central to neck difficulties that surfaced early in her life. Seven months after her conception, her neck was injured in the womb when her mother fell while running.

We return to 'My success hurts others.' Success in at least one aspect of the Japanese warrior's life — finding great love — had led not only to his own death by the sword, but also to the death of the woman he loved. Now that she is conscious of it, the threat of death from that disastrous event need no longer unconsciously pressure Maria when she achieves success.

By the end of this session, Maria is free of pain and feels lighter. Now that we have released some deep-seated anxieties, she begins to re-educate her mind with the affirmation, 'Success is safe for me! Success is my natural state!'

At first she cannot even say it. Soon she dissolves into gratitude for her creativity, for the beauty she can create — beauty she now sees can inspire others rather than trigger the jealousy her appearance and her creativity first attracted early in her childhood.

Such a session demonstrates how recurring thoughts can bring physical pain and lock chronic discord into a body.

Maria is soon tested. Before her next session she learns that an architect has chosen another of her designs for use, above those submitted by another student. She reports, 'I was very pleased, I thought, "Oh, that's great !" I felt a bit sad for the other student, but it just seemed normal that my work had been chosen.' She barely remembered her previous distress.

The above session may seem to have been chaotic until we realise that the healing dynamic of Maria's psyche linked her thoughts and feelings on a thread of emotional association, a function of the right brain hemisphere, rather than through the mental logic of left brain function.

Another illustration of this natural progression is the case of a woman taking her current sadness into a rebirthing session. She recalls a childhood memory of her father slapping her hard across the face. This triggers temporary facial twitching that leads back to facial contortions in the birth canal caused by cord strangulation — and foetal sadness at being hurt unfairly, which dissolves into a past-life drama on the same theme.

Inner work of this kind goes beyond words, into opening of heart feelings and spiritual sensing. It is more than managing stress or adjusting behaviour. It is true growth.

OPPORTUNITIES FOR CHANGE

In his book *Embracing Heaven and Earth,* Dr Hal Stone comments that holistic medicine views physical symptoms as opportunities to change consciousness for the better. And metaphysical author Jane Roberts in *Seth Speaks* denies that suffering is 'good for the soul' — unless it teaches us to stop suffering.

In my practice, clients focusing on other problems in both private and group sessions have reported rapid improvement in skin ailments, muscular tensions, gastritis, colitis, chronic or recent pain, inflammation, swelling, soreness and various other interruptions to health. Phobias (see Chapter Eight) and nervous breakdowns, with their distressing physical effects, have yielded relatively quickly in particular cases. Minor allergic reactions, frequently associated with past-life stories, sometimes clear up over a few breathing sessions without even addressing them or understanding how the shift has happened.

In achieving physical release of stress, past-life work not only deals with negative past programming — suggestions we have accepted as truth that don't work for us — but also with blocked bioenergies. Bioenergies are the living energy systems connected with the body. For decades, medical science has acknowledged that we are electromagnetic beings, and has scanned and measured electrical energy travelling through our brains, hearts, muscles. A number of instrumentation experiments of recent decades have detected and examined the energy field, or aura, surrounding the human body.

As new literature on bioenergies and this Einsteinian view of vibrational living systems is available in general bookshops, I simply mention it here as offering a probable explanation of the mechanics of past-life work. Given Professor Tiller's theories, that we store our past lifetime memories within our energy field, and that this field has an impact on, and even creates, our bodies, we cannot confine past lifetimes counselling to the mind only.

In a 1994 survey of past lifetimes therapists, writer Diane Goldner reported in the award-winning American magazine *New Age Journal*, that many people involved with past lifetimes therapy have told of spontaneous healings and psychological transformations which, she says, surpass results from mainstream medicine or psychoanalysis.

When past-life therapy is followed by release of a physical ailment, a profound question arises. Has the ailment been the result of a real or a fantasised trauma? We can't prove either.

Nevertheless, increasing numbers of mainstream practitioners are adopting the modality. In 1988, after Yale Medical School psychiatrist Dr Brian L.Weiss began practising past-life therapy, he wrote a book on one patient's regression journey, *Many Lives, Many Masters*. This has sold more than a million copies worldwide and has been translated into 23 languages. In 1994, his waiting list for regression therapy numbered 2000.

EASING MINDS OR BODIES

Part of the growing appeal of past-life work is that any problem lays itself open to the past lifetime lens.

Barrenness

In a breathwork session, a mature woman is embarrassed to report that she feels she is a large female animal. She describes leathery hooves. The animal watches its young walking about. Feeling the animal's maternal instincts, the woman experiences sudden strong pain in her own ovaries, and bursts into tears. 'Why don't I have children?' she sobs. The ovary pain subsides.

Why was an animal the agent for this moment of truth? Had she once been this animal? Through some hidden biological connection, her body responded to unbidden and unremarkable images, and began to release a deep hurt she normally masked.

Barrenness sometimes spurs a woman to explore her soul history. Where a woman says, 'I'm not good enough to have children', deep guilt can be a factor. Perhaps this is a conviction that she would make a dangerous mother — as where someone might discover that, in another age, she had made a living by killing her community's unwanted children.

Such a woman might say, 'I know if I hadn't, someone else would have, but my arms still feel contaminated, they shouldn't hold a baby.' She will have amassed guilt in this life also. The past-life story would point out the necessity of learning to forgive herself, to make true the affirmation, 'I love myself, no matter what.'

Asthma and Speech Difficulties.
People who develop asthma or speech inhibitions early in this life may later recall having been hanged or strangled in other lives — as well as suffering birth complications from having the umbilical cord wrapped around their neck.

Physical Addictions
Investigating physical addiction history often brings to light addiction in other lifetimes. A step out of drug addiction for a student of mine, a paramedic, was to relive the misery of a New York Bowery derelict. The 'black hole' she felt she was in largely belonged to this alcoholic, a former businessman whose entire family had been killed in a car accident. Her achievement in locating some of her depression where it belonged, in the past, and in letting go of it, lightened her own life.

The conduit of the 'black hole' terror from past to present life was a stage of her own birth in which she imprinted with the thought, 'There's no way out', which had also been the attitude of the derelict. Breathing out this birth trauma residue cleared more past stress, as well as drug residue, from her body.

Roots of drug addiction may jump centuries. Past lives highlight the ignorant use in former times of addictive drugs, such as laudanum, a derivative of opium, prescribed for many in the Victorian years as a tranquilising medicine. A few people have regressed to lives as priestesses holding the important office of oracle in ancient countries such as Greece. To enhance clairvoyance for the demands of the populace, a Greek oracle either lived over ground fissures that released underground gases or ingested drugs from plants. Such people in this life may suffer from 'spaciness' and be drawn to drugs, as well as being psychically developed.

Addiction to altered states of consciousness may have other roots. A compulsive marijuana user regressed to a hermit life of *madi*, or God intoxication, seen by his contemporaries as a form of madness.

Depression

The profound condition of misery often identified as 'the long dark night of the soul', as St. John of the Cross described it, is discovered through rebirthing to be an acting out of the 'No Exit' stage of birth mentioned above. This is literally a time of suffering. The cervix is closed, yet the foetus needs to move on out. There is literally no way out of the dark confining womb, until the cervix finally opens.

Past lifetime impressions coincidental with these feelings involve dungeons, situations of being trapped and of inescapable, looming death. I believe that past-life work, as well as rebirthing, has assisted many people to move past a point of possible suicide associated with this condition.

This offers hope, especially to young people. Australia has close to the highest youth suicide rate in the world. More than 400 people under 24 years of age kill themselves here annually, and many more make the attempt. A 1995 survey shows one in eight Australian schoolchildren are at risk of suicide. Suicide is the biggest cause of death for Australians under 30, with males most at risk.

Skin Problems

Holistic research reveals that skin problems can be associated with hidden anger. A man unaware that he was angry about the deaths of family members was plagued with full-body eczema. A past self of his blurted, 'My family's been murdered, and I'm burning up with anger!'

KIRSTI'S STORY

A recurring skin rash brought Kirsti, a beautiful young German woman, for sessions. She was secretly convinced she was ugly. She knew her belief was connected with the rash, which had begun three days after birth. Devastating skin outbreaks had persisted through teenage years into adulthood. She said, 'I get really scared of people looking at me.'

Kirsti first relived a past-life story of a crippled child suffering from boils, considered so ugly that when exorcism failed to cure her, she was forced to live in a forest out of people's sight. After this story came to awareness the condition slowly started to clear up. 'For a while I felt really beautiful,' said Kirsti.

Two years later, she released another layer of the problem by reliving a life as a beautiful woman raped by a man who, she felt, had reincarnated as her present mother. ('When I was little I was afraid of my mother.') After the rape, the woman 'felt so dirty' that in shame she joined a convent.

When Kirsti returned to Germany another attack hospitalised her. Antibiotics cleared it up. 'But,' she said when she was back in Australia, 'that was not getting to the cause.'

The small boy who now comes to her awareness is Indian, named Ma-gan, alive around AD 300. He is a beautiful child, petted and loved by his rich mother, who calls him 'my little prince'. But war strips away his mother's wealth, and she takes him to a cave before disappearing from his life.

Years later, Ma-gan finds himself caught up in the raucous sounds, the pungent smells of a bazaar. He is hungry, unhappy, dirty and alone. He thinks, 'I don't have any place in the world.'

Next he feels terror, hears a tiger growl in a forest, thinks, 'Is this how I have to die?' The tiger springs and crunches on his head. But Ma-gan does not die. Strangers help him. Badly scarred ('I don't look very good') he lives on to become a soldier fighting in a Holy War. He kills many of the enemy but eventually is assailed by a new feeling: 'This is not right!'

Later, to atone, he becomes a monk, happily walking far among people whose custom is to give him food in exchange for blessings. In kindness, he touches many poor and diseased people. His hands then develop boils that spread over his body. His belief is, 'I have to suffer because I killed so many people, I can't forgive myself.' While dying in agony from a swelling sickness in a cave he sings, still helping others around him.

After Ma-gan's death, I ask his spirit the lesson of that life: 'To love, to express my heart unconditionally.' After further completion work Kirsti, in visualisation, watches Ma-gan disappear into a realm of light. She has released more of her belief that she is ugly.

THE VISIBLE UNCONSCIOUS

Psychologist Dr Gina Cerminara, who wrote books about Edgar Cayce's 40-year psychic ministry, likened the human body to a book telling an individual's secret history. The body has also been called 'the visible unconscious'.

More examples from my casebook hint that the body is a bearer of coded messages:

* A woman with congenital kidney weakness relives being a boy whose father hits him across the kidneys with a chair.

* A man develops a fistula in a blood vessel behind his eyes. This is a deep ulcer that can appear in response to damage such as a gunshot wound, which he had not experienced. In session he feels he is a primitive tribesman appalled by the overbearing behaviour of white intruders. When he remonstrates, a white man shoots him in the face. (Such physical manifestations commonly appear when the present self is around the same age as the past self was when he or she suffered the trauma.)

* A man, fearing that unexplained chest pains herald a heart attack despite medical opinion to the contrary, relives being an Asian warlord. This barbarian enjoys a rough, happy and successful life. He dies unexpectedly from a heart attack, feeling cheated of more happiness. After recall, and expression of the anger, the man's current chest pains stop.

'WHY DID I HAVE THIS BACK PAIN?'

Even when an ailment has been removed, perhaps by surgery, looking into the past may settle the nagging question, 'Why did that happen to me?'

Evan came to me because of puzzling mental images. Lately he had been 'seeing' in his mind a picture, hanging on a wall, of a Tiger Moth aeroplane. He could remember neither picture nor plane. As we invited any relevant connections to come to awareness, he reported that his stomach muscles tensed.

Evan soon feels he is Albert, an English pilot in World War 1, who has killed 11 of the enemy. Sent on a reconnaissance mission over France, Albert spots the rural factory target from the air. Gazing down on oxen pulling carts between barren vineyards, he sees from the corner of his eye a German plane.

'God, where did he come from? Now, he's on my tail — he's a good pilot — I can't do anything — I'm turning left — God, I should have turned right — oh, no ...' Albert feels bullets rip through the plane into his back. 'It feels just like someone's kicked me in the back.' He's aware of the plane spinning out of control, brown leather around him, flight instruments, the smell of fuel — and later, of the roots of trees around him while the German plane circles above the wreck. Evan sees Albert's smashed body.

At first Evan is cut off from any depth of emotion,insisting that Albert's dying thoughts are, 'It's no big deal. I had a great life. I'll just come back and do it again.' But as we explore, he connects a little more to this past reality. 'An ambulance like a T-model Ford has to leave the road to get to my body. They just toss it in, take it to a stone building. Lots of bodies here. Don't put me with the soldiers, I'm an airman! There's a couple of fly-boys here.'

As I guide Albert's spirit to move on, regret and sadness swamp him. 'I never finished anything!' Albert cries. 'And I should have turned right, I made a fatal mistake!'

Evan was born prematurely, by Caesarean section. Therefore he did not finish his womb life or his birth journey, and later had trouble finishing other things. He was fathered by a perfectionist who severely punished mistakes. Albert was shot in the back and died weighed down with having made a mistake. Evan carried severe back pain for 25 years, until an operation corrected the condition.

CAN THE BODY ANTICIPATE?

Sometimes it seems as though the body can anticipate opportunity to resolve latent discord. A week before a regression workshop, an intending participant developed severe earache. A doctor prescribed antibiotics but she decided not to take them. On workshop day, she tried to ignore acute pain through the morning's group preparation. In the afternoon, she was guided to impressions of the distant past. At the end of regression, her ear immediately improved — by next morning it was normal. What had dissolved the ear pain?

She had glimpsed two lives: 'First I felt I was a man, a pirate on board ship. One leg had gangrene. I was drinking to ease the pain. I was banging the side of my head against the mast because that pain was easier to bear than the pain of the leg. My shipmates carried me ashore in Calcutta for help. The sights I saw going through the streets were so terrible that I was overwhelmed. I died on the stretcher.'

In the second life she was again a man: 'Arabs had stolen my children. I chased one on horseback, he hit me with a sword. While I was lying on the hot sand — I could feel sand in my mouth — I felt a kick from a boot on my right ear. That was the last I knew in that life.'

We go to the cinema to see movies like these. It seems we've lived our own movies. (And we're doing it right now!)

PREVENTATIVE HEALTHCARE?

I suspect that past-life work can also be utilised as preventive healthcare.

A healthy woman seeking to change deep behavioural patterns uncovers six past lives in which each past self suffered serious head injury, from a variety of causes. Is this pointing to a hidden weakness in her present body?

As well as releasing unconscious stress from these physical shocks, her inner work has done much to resolve the emotional problems of those lifetimes. Has she thereby been neutralising a predisposition to head injury this time around?

In my past lifetimes counselling training courses, I guide trainees in an experimental session on 'the past lifetime most threatening my future health in this life'. Trainees have thus had the opportunity to resolve some stressful situations in past lives —but we cannot document the results of this experiment !

In spite of the growing successes of past-life work, I feel that the modality is still in its infant stages. Opportunity for research and development in the coming century is enhanced by the fact that, when the work is done thoroughly, there are no negative side effects, only bonuses.

TITANIC

Our emotional state around birth relates to how our biological clocks set themselves in the first hours of life, governing innate functions such as lifelong reactions to air temperature changes. Our emotional state around birth seems often to be influenced by our emotional state during a previous death.

A woman wanted to find out why she always described her overreaction to cold as "I have ice water in my veins." She put this together with a lifelong fascination with the story of the sinking of the *Titanic*, a new luxury passenger liner that sank long before she was born, in collision with icebergs in 1912. She was puzzled, as she now has no fear of drowning or of the sea.

Her story was of a young Irish boy who stowed away on the liner to make a new life in America. Caught, he was put to work with others in the bowels of the ship shovelling coal into the boilers. When the ship struck the iceberg he drowned, trapped in the freezing waters that invaded the hull.

She reported later that week that her husband, who loved to cuddle up to her in sleep, reported that he'd had to move away because she was too hot. Something had changed, after one session. Hopefully, the two of them adjusted!

Chapter Eight

Fear

Regression story from Prue, a nurse:
All the villagers are talking about young John. He's a cheerful boy obsessed with watching birds fly, leaves fall. He twirls sticks and leaves into the air. People in this 13th-century English village don't have much entertainment and so they enjoy John, especially when he jumps out of trees with out-stretched arms.

When he announces his great ambition they fall about laughing. 'People can't fly!' they howl, slapping one another. Some laugh till they cry at the stick-and-leaf models from the mind of a madman. But they humour him, eager for his next trick. And he has a way about him — all that enthusiasm.

In his twenties, John has an idea so wonderful that he turns cartwheels. He knows how to make his dreams come true! He rushes about explaining, cajoling, drawing pictures in the dust of roads, fields and farmyards. The people co-operate. Soon he has a mounting pile of pieces of leather and tough scraps of the coloured fabrics they all wear. He organises volunteers to sew these together. They gossip and giggle for hours while they sew as John directs.

They've sewn a strange huge bag, and a harness, then fixed the two together. As John fits the harness on to himself they stagger about laughing. But John's so excited, inspecting the bag laid out behind him, braced open at one end, that he jumps up and down.

When a windy day arrives, the volunteers and their children and dogs go out to low grassy hills, a mile back from the sea, and stand around John as he lays out his multicoloured invention and puts on the harness. They help hold the fabric.

John stands tall in the wind. His face lifts to the blue sky where he so desperately longs to be. Then he begins to run. He runs and runs and runs, up and down the gentle slopes, straining muscles toughened by a life of farmwork. He drags the weight of the rising balloon behind him until the wind jabs tears from his eyes and his breath is like daggers in his chest. As he runs he shrieks to the wind to take him.

127

And the wind does. Running down a slope, John finds his legs running on air — for a few seconds. Falling back in a heap on the ground, he screams and drums his heels in triumph. For those seconds he had been a bird!

Then the villagers treat him with a touch more respect. But really, they say, all that fuss over a jump in the air. If God had meant men to fly, He'd have put feathers on their arms.

John's eyes glitter with his next plan. Obsessed, he repairs rips in the balloon and ambitiously announces the site of the next windy experiment: a clifftop high above the sea.

The villagers gather at the hill down which John will run to the cliff edge. He inspects the fabric, tests the harness and puts it on. Above the half-a-gale sea wind, he yells to the grinning people that this is the best moment in all his 27 years. The coloured bag blunders about on the ground behind him, snatching at their hands.

Once more he stands tall, facing out to sea. He breathes deeply of the buffeting wind, his friend. Certain of victory, he starts to run down the slope. The balloon begins to fill with air. John forces himself to run faster and faster against its pulling and swinging. He runs close to the high edge of land, ready to leap into flight.

Abruptly the wind whips about, shoves him sideways. He staggers, yanked by the balloon. Another sudden change of wind slaps him sharply and gusts against the now-collapsing balloon. John and the balloon fall off the cliff.

And he floats....he floats in the air for the briefest time, before the balloon flattens. John plummets like a rock all the way to the rocky bottom, landing on a thorn bush growing from a ledge. A long thorn pierces his eye and his brain.

In slow motion, the harlequin balloon crumples and folds down on top of the broken body impaled on the bush, a shroud frisked about by the fickle wind.

The people can't get down the cliff, so they leave him there.

John's story taps the dreams of countless unrecognised hero-inventors who courted flight in the many centuries before we could catch a plane to just about anywhere. They all shared the same magnificent urge as the Wright brothers. But they did not have the technological resources that enabled Orville and Wilbur Wright to invent their flying machine in 1903, or

Californian biologist Bryan Allen to pedal an aircraft weighing 75 pounds across the English Channel in 1979.

Prue, who recalled the balloon story with much emotion, had wanted to know why she felt so much fear of heights. Although John had shown no such fear beforehand, his gloriously confident cliff jump had ended in disaster. As Prue and I worked with the ingredients of John's story, a measure of fear left her.

Whether or not we consciously remember, deep present fears often seem to be caused by violence in the distant past.

At times, fear is a lifesaver alerting us to danger. But at other times, fear is a life-quencher, a blanketing pall over our inborn ability to learn new things, try new actions, move out from the familiar to discover more of the world. Fear, like guilt, can become a habit that blocks growth, taught by one generation to the next. 'I'll only take a risk if it doesn't ruffle anyone's feathers,' says a woman who'd learned early at home that ruffling feathers brought trouble. Another remembers parental admonishment, 'Sit still or I'll murder you!'

Fear can also be a runaway bully, an apparently irrational master distressing our bodies with panic symptoms, flooding us with shame and crippling our confidence to deal with daily life.

Excessive, inappropriate fear — phobia — commonly concerns water, flying, public speaking, enclosed spaces, being outdoors, darkness, insects, birds, fire, violence and death. What sets off phobia symptoms can be something as ordinary as seeing a cockroach, hearing a flock of birds, or getting into a lift.

Phobias of needles or knives ('of a sharp object injuring my eyes') may well be birth-related, referring to the obstetrician's scalpel in Caesarean births, or episiotomy, or a forceps delivery. In such cases, stabbing or instrument torture in past lives seems linked. Other phobia triggers reported to me have included loud sounds, synthesiser music, the noise of breaking glass, peeling skin, blonde blue-eyed women, 'high whistling wind', the thought 'of being under a train', and 'deep water, as in a fall from an ocean liner'. Other people's panic attacks have been triggered by any mention of illness, or when walking down steps, or needing to sign documents.

Phobic reaction can escalate from a thudding heart and sweating, to uncontrollable trembling, dizziness, fainting, vomiting, and pain. Reactions are compounded by confusion and shame, for one of the terrors that people with phobias suffer is that of being thought strange, even crazy. These sufferers can go to extraordinary lengths to avoid situations that bring up their fear — which means that fear controls parts of their lives. Some fears can so debilitate people that they live as prisoners in their own homes, sometimes in their beds.

Extreme fear of failure, or of other people's judgements, can escalate to suicide. Fear of success can condemn a person to poverty. Fear of relating intimately can stunt a life.

Yet fears and phobias are not necessarily a life sentence.

WATER PHOBIA

The nurse who recalled the balloon story is a warm, capable woman who has helped many people, including her husband and three children, now adult. Although dealing with medical crises that would daunt other people, she feared heights and also water. Prue had never been able to put her face into water, not even under the shower. All her life she had avoided swimming and being in boats. Fear governed a number of her choices living, as she does in an Australian city on a river, near the sea.

Like other people with phobias, Prue had struggled valiantly to overcome her terror through willpower, trying to fight something unseen that could reduce her to horror and helplessness. Unaccountably, the phobia sufferer panics, even sobs — as though death awaits. Perhaps, once, it did. Not that time when three-year-old Prue was dumped by a large wave. Nor that other time when, as a child, she struggled to pull her sister out of a tidal rip. But...

Now Prue and I aim to find a past lifetime incident so rich in inner significance for her that stripping it of its emotional charge may also defuse her continuing water crises. A powerful other-life story emerges:

Regression: My name is Ann, I'm a teenager in the Middle Ages. Animals are attracted to me, I put my hands on them. I lay my hands on sick people too. They get better. The villagers become frightened of me, call me a witch. They capture me, dress me in black, line up on the bank of the pond to watch me die on a ducking stool. They strap me tightly into the seat, around my

130

waist and my back. They swing the stool over the deep part of the pond. They hold the seat under until I'm dead.

Sadly, Prue draws a picture of this antique torture instrument shaped like a seesaw hung from a frame, showing which parts were wood, which leather, as though its construction were burned on her memory. It was the last object Ann saw. Prue, the modern healer, comments with tears in her eyes, 'She was drowned for loving.'

Yet Ann's terror was not the prime key to Prue's phobia. She still could not face water.

Some time later, at a rebirthers' training course, Prue courageously attempted wet rebirthing. This is a technique in which the supported breather lies face down in water, breathing through a snorkel for an hour or so. The process gently, but powerfully, assists people spontaneously to re-experience the start of a major negative pattern. Responses to stress such as 'I can't get started', 'I can't get through', or 'I can't do it' could well have been seeded during gestation or birth. The aim is to release emotional charge from the pattern, to free up its bound energy via naturally oxygenating body and brain. This triggers biochemicals which activate the limbic system, associated with emotions.

Prue refused to begin easily. I watched with compassion as, helped by a partner, she failed a number of times to lie face down in shallow water and breathe. Once when she jumped up choking she gasped, 'I feel I'm drowning.'

Intuitively I asked, 'What is your name?' The surprising reply was 'Jason'.

While Prue crouched trembling in the water we briefly explored the new story emerging into awareness. Jason was a 15-year-old British seaman who had drowned off a raft after a shipwreck. It began to seem as though whenever Prue's face touched water, she relived Jason's drowning.

Separating herself from the Jason energy was a wrench for Prue, who at the last minute instinctively said, 'But I won't be able to do anything without him.' Although this was her first conscious awareness of his presence, I took this to mean that the blockage in her life energy had been with her from birth or before. This would be logical, if reincarnation were true.

She decided it was time she moved on from the crippling situation. She took the plunge of letting Jason go. In her inner

131

vision she allowed him to go up into light, guided by a spiritual being of his choice, until he vanished.

She immediately took the plunge again, into the water. This time she glided in face down, smoothly and happily, probably for the first time in her life. She breathed submerged through the snorkel for 15 minutes. She told us excitedly, 'That felt wonderful!' Three days later she was thrilled to enjoy a swimming pool, and to receive her first lesson in the Australian crawl, which requires the face to be in water.

On the evidence of Prue's transformation, which has lasted, and that of others who have freed themselves similarly, who is to say that phobias are irrational? Surely it is reasonable to be terrified of something that once traumatised and/or killed you — even if the event occurred 300 or 3000 years ago — until you finish your emotional or transpersonal business with the original situation, as Prue did.

Approaching fears and phobias through past lifetime stories can enlist healing powers latent within oneself. Understanding what causes a phobia is not enough to release it, although it may give hope. The original memory must be found, faced and felt, in a safe way, before the emotional/physical charge can dissolve.

Dr John Lilley likens negative patterns buried in the subconscious to 'downer programs that have been embedded in (our) computers'. Long-time American consciousness researcher, author, pioneer in interspecies communication, and inventor of the float tank, Dr Lilley has personally engaged in inner exploration over decades. He stated in the 'eighties, 'Everyone has the potential to dig away at these programs and get rid of them.'

FEARFUL DREAMS

Sometimes childhood nightmares can later be recognised as glimpsed memories of terrors from other lives. Frightening dreams always have powerful messages for us, especially if they recur.

Marion is a financial consultant. As a child she suffered recurring dreams of horror and violence, of rushing horses, a river, and swinging blades. In session now she sees the face of a man from those dreams, a blond, blue-eyed man to whom she is strangely drawn, although she feels she has never met him in this life. As a story unfolds, Marion is swept into intense emotions.

Regression : *I'm a slave, a young female, in a group of slaves. I see a man working with horses, I feel instant attraction to him, it just hits me. I'm in love! He's attracted to me too. It's so strong.*

He smuggles me into another group by disguising me. I work in the palace kitchens. We can be together.

But the king takes a fancy to me. He fits me out with a gold slave choker and a chain, treats me like a pet. He's a big man, piggish, brutal, a real despot. The king finds out about my lover and imprisons him. He tells me he's going to boil him in oil. I'm frantic. Secretly I get keys and let him out. We escape.

We get to a river by dusk. ('I always get sad at dusk.') We're free, but we realise there's nowhere for us to go. We cling to each other. Now there are horsemen coming, huge horses are thundering up to us, we're on the ground. There's the king, swinging a big sword. There's no hope for us. The king charges up to me and slashes me through the heart. As he hacks into our bodies I hear him shout, 'We'll meet again!'

Marion feels she recognises the king as a present-day employer who acts like a despot and has told her she is the girl of his dreams. Marion is repelled. She says, 'I feel the clutch of déjà vu. I feel in the power of a ruthless man who'd stop at nothing.' The distant memory strengthens her resolve not to become a victim of this entity again.

COMMON FEARS

Although you may not suspect distant past sources, you may be aware of holding strong fears. Perhaps the fear is of expressing intense feelings, or you may fear change, going to sleep, being a woman, or a man. People going through new stages of inner development may fear 'going mad'.

The present Extreme fear of facing the present can trigger a stress response of 'I have to get out of here', creating a leaving pattern that erupts when relationships and other normal situations become difficult.

The future Fear of facing the future can block off possibilities of expansion and growth.

The past Fear of facing the past results in stockpiled emotional baggage. It often includes fear of even thinking about one's birth. When fear is buried as far back as birth, or in utero, it is sure to be so basic that it has always constricted an individual. A relatively small amount of time spent re-experiencing birth may free up all the years ahead.

To release deep-seated fear we need to respect the sometimes bewildering machinations of the mind. Painful material might first appear in inner vision in unrelated flashes, even in cartoon form. And the practitioner needs to respect the traveller's tolerance threshold, even though the traveller is free at all times to say 'Stop'.

In session, creeping up on fearful situations might involve first taking a quick glance, as though at a movie, then taking a time leap to later and looking back on a crisis, and, finally, when some initial fear has dissipated, returning to just before the event and re-experiencing it once, then several times, to drain its emotional content, or energy.

Occasionally, my clients choose to continue living with an inner handicap rather than to clear a memory. And sometimes a person needs deep hypnosis to remove conscious control, to work through issues that resist other states of consciousness.

We see, then, that fears belonging in the past do not always stay in the past. Fears gathered in the current life can be exaggerated by burdens of fear brought in from other lives, whether these are ancient, or as recent as earlier in this century. For example, many people discover they are carrying fears from terrible events their past selves experienced in one of the two World Wars. These situations respond to help from the present self, restoring the ability to live more confidently in the present moment.

This is a practical and wise step to take, because fears tend to attract experiences of a similar order, as the Biblical Job bewailed: 'The thing that I feared most has come upon me!' We seem to magnetise to us what we focus on.

In a state of metaphysical unconsciousness we clear these fears slowly, by living through a series of similar occurrences, even lifetimes, without awareness of an overall pattern. But these days, through such techniques as past lifetimes resolution, we can clear the patterns faster.

DO WE NEED TO BE VICTIMS?

In this life, as well as others, we have probably all been victims to some degree at some time - even perhaps terrorised and in desperate need of compassion and help. This is a situation most of us would never want to be in again.

Within Western society, some people are questioning the concept of being a victim. Psychological studies of the thoughts, feelings and behaviour of victims focus attention on the power of our beliefs and attitudes to determine our life experience.

For example, in experiments, muggers have identified from a number of photographs of unknown people those they are likely to attack, or to avoid. It seems they instinctively read subtle unconscious messages people broadcast through body language and appearance. You may know someone who habitually slouches as though expecting to be hit — probably because as a child, he or she often was.

Now there are indications that, however terrible our experiences may have been, perhaps victims do not need to remain in a victim state. Researchers are exploring concepts which initially seem absurd, but reveal personal interactions below the level of awareness. They suggest the existence of unconscious contracts around violence: 'I'll attack you and you'll let me.' For the victim, this can involve hidden pay-offs in being frightened, robbed, hurt, even cursed, to 'validate' deep beliefs that others, or life, or even God, are out to get them. Such imprints often begin at birth. To discover this pattern in ourselves may be painful, but it brings a reward. Once we know what is happening, we can do something about it.

This approach explores whether we unconsciously manifest situations out of deeply held beliefs, such as 'People hurt me', and also out of past lifetime patterns of victimhood. While humans as a race may never surmount the problem, many individuals now engaged in systematic self-discovery do surmount their fears and deal with hidden aspects of themselves which they feel have attracted violence, as they learn to own more of their personal power. This takes courage.

An instance in which past lifetimes counselling helped to turn the victim syndrome around involved a woman clearing a lifelong pattern of victimisation, particularly in relationships. She had for two years felt in her back, a burning sensation which had not responded to any treatment. I asked her to picture a symbol for the sensation. She sensed a bishop's crook.

This symbol unlocked a life story of a Spanish bishop. Up to then, Christina had dealt with several past lives as a victim, including being a Cathar burned to death. This bishop was a member of the Spanish Inquisition. He personally sent hundreds of Cathars to burn, and tortured many others.

Christina said, 'I had a lot of reluctance and self-disgust around getting to understand the bishop as a past self of mine. But a powerful past-life session eventually revealed the whole story. At 10, this person had been a victim himself, abandoned to a religious institution by his parents and sexually abused by older boys. The one moment of his life I resonated to was when he was a choirboy, desperately singing his heart out to God.

'As an adult, the bishop's genuine belief was that he must exorcise the Devil through these heretics, and it was exaggerated by a compulsion for revenge. Resolving the issues resulted in an amazing healing. The burning energy on my back disappeared and has not returned.'

Perhaps even more importantly, this resolution of a victim/aggressor theme deep in her psyche seemed a vital step for Christina in letting go of an unsuitable marriage and taking new career steps that have dissolved even more of her former victim state.

PERSECUTION OF NATURAL HEALERS
Stories of persecution such as that of Cathars, or Prue's death by ducking stool for being a sensitive, are not unusual distant memories. My files bulge with recalled stories of persecution of natural healers. Through the ages, others who did not understand their abilities were frightened by them, even though their own sick friends and relatives and even persecutors themselves had often regained health through the ministrations of such folk herbalists, touch-practitioners, clairvoyants, midwives. This early doctoring utilised diagnostic and health-improving processes and systems well known and respected today, including visualisation and alpha brainwave techniques that have been taught worldwide for many years to great numbers of people, especially in the field of business.

The last witchcraft trial occurred as recently as 1944, in England. A highly respected psychic medium, Helen Duncan, was jailed under the *Witchcraft Act of 1735* — sparking a protest from Winston Churchill on the waste of public funds. In 1951, this Act was replaced by the *Fraudulent Mediums Act*, which legally recognised as charities Spiritualist churches, with their mediumistic ministers.

Natural healers in past-life regressions uniformly express a passionate devotion to their ministry. One such past 'heretic' self, urged by her fearful mother to stop having visions and laying hands on the sick, explained, 'I can't not do it.' She was imprisoned at age 23, dragged naked by horses over the stony ground of a sporting arena, and then eviscerated, alive.

Small wonder that Lauren, who regressed to that life, had never felt energy in her hands until it flowed after the regression. It seems that fear had inhibited the life force. 'I feel different,' she said, remarking on buzzing sensations in her hands.

Where once the Church felt threatened by natural healers, now there are other established institutions challenged by the public demand for alternative healing methods. The growing trend is indicated in a study by Harvard Medical School, showing that in out-of-pocket payments, Americans' spending on alternative healing techniques rivals their spending on hospitalisation. In Australia, in October 1994, *The Bulletin* proclaimed that up to 40% of Australians preferred to use alternative medical services. By 1996, Australians were spending nearly $1 billion a year on alternative treatments, according to *The Lancet* medical journal. A modern difference is that many medical practitioners as well as consumers consider emerging modalities to be complementary rather than alternative to mainstream health practices.

People who recall past stories of persecution as healers are often themselves now working in a healing profession, orthodox or alternative — or wishing to do so. By eliminating fears from the past, when their healing activities brought them hardship, torture or death, these people find new confidence in presenting their gifts to a needy community, in both orthodox and alternative fields.

OTHER COMMON FEARS

Fear of parents Excessive childhood fear of one's parents is one of the most paralysing fears, because children dependent on their parents are at their mercy. And the fear is ever present in the family home. Adults sometimes recall that in their childhood homes, savage beltings were 'normal', or 'I slept every night with a blanket over my head, scared my father would kill me in the night', or they were constantly sexually abused, or subjected to cruel whims of parents who were frequently drunk. Even when adulthood minimises the fears, their reverberations remain in attitude to life.

Such intensity in any situation signals the possibility of extra charge from past-life situations, that can be made available to such adults as keys for change. These past stories are not pretty. They often occurred when no recourse such as police or humane laws or welfare agencies existed.

Fear of being buried alive In session numbers of my clients express the fear of being buried alive. Surely nobody would relish this. But as a recurring fear, it adds claustrophobic tension to daily life. Fear of smothering, or being unable to breathe, may be so vivid that a person cannot stand any covering over the head, face or eyes. This may trace back to being shut in a cupboard as a child, being covered by a blanket as an infant, being oxygen-deprived in utero, and so on.

Entombment through accident, custom or murder has occurred often in history. Such situations can surprise us during regression. Memory of a taste in the mouth — perhaps the taste of boar soup drunk in a draughty castle — can catapult someone into recalling the trauma of being walled up by an enemy soon after the meal.

We can also look to legitimate burial before a person is dead. Even today, judging stages of death can be difficult. There is clinical death, biological death and brain death. And now many cases have been documented where people apparently dead returned to life — hours, occasionally days, after death was pronounced. On the video *Visions of Hope*, in which people recount their near-death experiences, an Englishman tells of how he revived on a slab in a hospital morgue, hours after being pronounced dead. (He said that as his mother had always taught him to care for others, he got up and fetched the collapsing morgue attendant a drink.)

Fear of Meditative States of Consciousness A number of people have come to me to release blocks to going deeper into meditation or relaxation. They do not feel afraid, yet are unable to reach these states.

138

The blocks have to do with unrecognised fear of accepting more of their intuitive, emotional and creative capacities. This results in personality imbalance, instanced in the extreme by the purely rational individual, in whom these right-brain functions seem frozen.

Causes have been various, but they always involve fear of accessing deeper states of consciousness than are required in daily living. Present-life conditioning at school and at home against daydreaming and introspection ('wasting time') has echoed more serious prohibitions from past lives, such as contemplative lifestyles that have led to disaster, or intuitive abilities that have been punished.

Hiding beneath such a block, a businessman uncovered the following: 'I feel as though I have a band around my middle, two ropes stretching above me, two rough men holding them, pulling me about. It's awful. Something black, sticky. I see clear blue. I feel nausea, rage, throat constriction, pain, a huge yearning.' He flashed briefly to his own infancy, to similar feelings while straining at a harness held by his mother. In a sudden movement, he appeared to pull a belt off over his head. 'I'm sinking now. I feel peace.' He smiled.

To me these impressions suggested memories of being keelhauled under a tarred ship's bottom, with changes of consciousness related to drowning. Whenever the man felt himself deeply relaxing in meditation, an automatic switch would cut in and send him either to sleep, or back towards the waking state, to protect him from recall of this suffering.

I asked if his impressions reminded him of a possible event in history. He said no. I said, 'How about keelhauling?' He shuddered. 'No,' he said, 'I'm only shuddering because I've seen it on television and it was horrible, I felt sick.' The body tells the tale that the conscious mind shuts out. But whatever the impressions represented, by becoming aware of them he was already starting to clear the block.

Fear of Public Speaking One of the most common fears is fear of public speaking, or of being the focus of a group. Through individual investigation, such fears prove to be grounded in past embarrassment or harassment in groups, either family groups or larger. Incidents may or may not be readily remembered. One recognisable source of this fear is having been publicly ridiculed or abused at school, or in kindergarten.

Amazingly, imprints of shame and fear in front of others are frequently traced to birth, our first performance. Perhaps our body felt, or was, distorted ('ugly') after the passage through the birth canal. Perhaps someone at our delivery made a disparaging remark about our appearance. Remember that research shows that while babies can't understand words, they are incredibly sensitive to emotional atmosphere, a startling idea that many people have discovered was true for them.

Or perhaps, as others have found, the first time we used our voice was in front of a delivery team when a well-meaning doctor physically attacked us by smacking us to make us breathe — and somehow we still expect that public exposure will result in shock, pain, betrayal and humiliation.

Another factor is, if we have not cleared negative patterning from our childhood, we can unconsciously set up an audience to represent our parents in disapproving mode, and expect, and sometimes get, the worst.

Clearing trauma from present-life experiences can help relieve performance anxiety. But often there are deeper influences at work as well. Throughout human history individuals have been terrorised by mobs, usually for breaking social rules. Perhaps a former self stole, had forbidden sex, fraternised with enemies, or was just different. The horror of being stoned to death by a mob or purposely killed before a hostile crowd jumps centuries, and such stories turn up frequently in my consulting room. Reliving them can in fact be an adventure, because it can transmute fear of public performance into excitement, as old habits of reaction are dropped.

PANIC IN FRONT OF GROUPS

Panic attacks were disrupting Willa's life. They came less often after some rebirthing sessions, but she still felt ill and breathless in groups of people larger than eight, even if they were all her friends. If there were men in the group, laughing, she'd expect to be hurt, and would feel a spinning sensation. All through her childhood she had panicked in queues or crowded shops ('in case I would fall flat on my face').

As we tracked this panic over several visits, Willa re-experienced her birth. She said, 'I don't want to get out of the womb because people hurt me.' Perhaps she learned this when turned manually in the womb into a correct pre-birth position. Although she consciously saw no connection between that event and her adult life, Willa described dissatisfaction with her non-assertiveness in these words: "I pass on the decision-making to someone else because I don't do anything about it, then I see myself being pushed into a position.' She also said: 'I feel my husband manipulates me.'

Willa seemed to learn that people hurt her before she was turned in the womb, in lifetimes where she was publicly burned at the stake, and, as a 12th-century Macedonian priest, was hanged by people hostile to his teachings.

Another fear trigger was oriental music. A regression opens in her inner vision on a hot day with a view of mountains. 'I've climbed them,' she says. 'They're so high, they take your breath away.'

Regression: My home is big brown tents on yellow sand, green and red cushions everywhere. The people travel on camels. We're moving camp. I want to run away. ('I feel sick thinking about it.')

A favourite time in that childhood was playing with my brothers, tumbling around the tent. My mother's a little lady, pretty, in flowing robes, a veil, jewellery. She loves me, calls me her golden jewel. I'm the youngest girl. My father is a kind man in flowing robes, he talks with other men. My mother's teaching me to dance, I like to dance but I don't because every-one looks at me, my brothers make fun of me.

But I have to dance later. When I'm 15 my father makes me leave the family, I don't want to. He trades me to a rich sheikh. I have to dance at a wild party. The sheikh makes love to me. I don't feel anything, he's just a smelly old man. I hate him, he made me leave home. He's got other wives.

Now I'm 20. I feel so irrelevant. I'm lying thinking, I'm scared and angry. This sheikh, I can't stand him. He's cruel. I think I'm going to kill him. I kill him with a sword.

A lot of his men are chasing me, laughing. They behead me.

As she contacts the shock, pain shoots through Willa's ear. Then she is flooded with insights. She recognises her fears and humiliation around being a girl, terrors of 'exposing herself' and dislike of men laughing in a group, and of the music endemic to that lifetime. She says, 'I'm always wanting to be level-headed!' Perhaps the severed head hit the floor face first — 'in case I would fall flat on my face'.

After working with these life stories, Willa reports less fear and more self-confidence. She soon achieves talking to a roomful of business associates while being filmed on video. 'It was no problem! That was amazing!' she reported.

To release outdated fears, people need to be ready. Some may never be ready to attempt this method. Others may be able to release only gradually, or the time may be right for massive improvement.

Chapter Nine

Exploring Past Lives by Yourself

Some people purposely explore their past lives alone or with friends, out of curiosity or as a spiritual practice — or to encourage spontaneous memories to continue unfolding in daily life. Exploring one's own consciousness is a natural activity, a birthright. We explore also through dreaming, daydreaming, imagining, reading, praying, meditating, remembering, being creative. These are some ways we activate, and even awaken, natural brain functions.

Books such as this one educate people that past-life journeys are not party tricks, as they can quickly become intensely personal. We have seen that, along with recalling mundane, revealing or inspirational experiences, travellers risk invoking memories that could frighten them and even temporarily stress their bodies — as can dreams. Yet our memories are our own. We're all entitled to them. Voluntary past lifetime exploring has been happening for years. Some people devoted to systematic self-realisation practices are willing to take the risk.

Because violence is regarded as a normal presence in millions of living rooms through the medium of television, tolerance of perceived trauma is marginally easier than it used to be. We live in a world where, before the average American child leaves primary school, he or she has seen up to 8000 murders acted out on television. Australians also view unpleasant events daily, which at least familiarises us with shocking situations.

If successful, solo exploration of past lifetimes can often be fragmentary and tentative, but it may also be powerful. If it happens to unlock grief, this is a blessing: a good cry now and again does us all a power of good. But if it distresses anyone more deeply, then professional assistance can usually be found somewhere for a serious healing crisis, because more practitioners are taking up this study.

However, I do offer advice to lone adventurers :

  * If you're scared before you start, don't do it.

143

* If fears come up during a journey, stop, and get professional assistance. As with any inner focusing, from meditation to daydreaming, occasional images can spark fear. One instance is imagery of a demon or devil. You can view these as personifications of your deep fears. Your unconscious is trying to grab your attention, as it does with 'bad' dreams.

An effective way to deal with fearful images is simply to command, 'Take off your mask!' until the image changes to a manageable one. A skeleton? See it as a pun. What are the 'bare bones' of an issue currently confronting you? 'Show me your message!' makes use of such previously frightening symbols.

* To clearly delineate between the past and the present, it is important to always conclude an inner journey with a formal wake-up suggestion, such as those on commercial audiotapes featuring past-life meditations. This could be: 'Soon I will count from five to one, and by the count of one I will be wide awake, feeling relaxed and refreshed. Five, four, three, two, one, WIDE AWAKE!'

* A traveller can further ground him or herself back in the present by immediately drawing and writing a record of the experience and what it signifies in the present, also by eating, drinking (not alcohol) and talking about the experience to a sympathetic listener or on audiotape.

Here is an account of one woman's solitary journeying, and its resonances in her everyday life.

STELLA'S STORY
Stella is a speech pathologist in her twenties:

It's hard now to recall a time when past lives were not part of my personal make-up. The richness of consciousness was never so evident as when I was delving into another part of myself.

My first experience of past-life work was through a 'do-it-yourself' regression tape. I happened to mention my intention of using the tape to a psychic, who issued dire warnings of danger and potential mental imbalance. But I find this notion somewhat off-balance — that I should live in fear and trepidation of the mind with which I spend all my waking and sleeping hours.

144

My first journeys were unremarkable glimpses into pasts that could be at best considered mundane and not at all the illuminating revelations that were likely to blow my mind away. Indeed, they did not even create a light breeze around my comfortable belief system.

The first set of images was of me as a foot soldier in ancient Rome, marching through mud. Through the monotonous rhythm of tired men marching, I happened to glance to my side and saw a man I recognised as my closest friend in those times — not a close bond, merely the association of two men who travel from war to war and bawdy house to bawdy house together. He's now a male friend in my present life. I rushed to the conclusion that no wonder my present male friend rarely, if ever, noticed I was female.

The other glimpse was one in war-torn Germany where as a girl I was raped by soldiers. Too much like a Hollywood movie script to be given much credence. And yet even now, many years after that brief flash, I cannot write of the incident with any of the flippancy one would expect if one's mind were just dredging up a movie.

Quite often now, my experiences of journeys into past lives take very much the format of a movie — technicolor visions that dance across my mind's eye with vivid realism, provoking deep emotion and with it, deep change. But then, in my early days of exploration, it was more like a mind game, an interesting diversion, rather like reading my weekly horoscope The change in my perception of the value of past lives happened in another unremarkable life of the past.

In my current life as a therapist, I was treating a large number of multiple sclerosis sufferers. My personal opinion then was that this disease, either by the changes it creates in the victim's brain, or by the inherent physical dependency it forces on its recipients, seemed to me to manifest a singularly dependent group of clients who *en masse* seemed to hand over all their personal power to anyone foolish enough to receive it. Harsh words? Yes, but heartfelt at the time.

My patience, which usually could be stretched to accommodate most of my clients, was becoming less and less evident in my relationship with these people. One weekend, I decided to use my tape to escape into a life that for a while would give me some relief from the stress I was feeling, and from my own

145

self-condemnation for being so intolerant. I requested of myself some insight into how I could cope with managing these people.

Regression: *The sun streams in through the window, dancing on my white tunic as I lie in bed. I can see the blue of the Mediterranean sparkling through the window. But I feel no joy, no satisfaction with what are obviously comfortable surroundings. I feel helpless, impotent, words can't describe the feelings of worthlessness and powerlessness. A rage swells inside me with no opportunity of physical release. I am paralysed, with a wasting disease that none of the doctors can diagnose or treat.*

I lie in my bed being cared for by my household, in particular a boy of eight in a tunic, and a young woman, who tend me. They are both so patient, so tender, so loving. I want to die. I had been a soldier in the Greek army, a man of enormous stature both physically and in leadership. I was much admired for my disciplined but fair management of my men. I tell the boy of battles and tales of foreign lands.

I've been a liberal, kind, firm bear of a man, much loved, and still in my illness much visited by friends and colleagues. I want to die, my whole illness and the care it entails is so undignified. And yet all the people who care for me and visit me treat me with all the respect and deference I've been accorded throughout my life. I am so humbled by the human compassion of those around me, so grateful.

I came out of my self-regression with tears streaming down my face. I had not followed my other self right through to his death. I left him with the duality of his life, the outer love and tolerance, and the inner rage, the anger for something better. I felt cleansed by the whole experience. I spent much quiet time refreshed by the encounter with a man who, although I'd had no experience of him in his prime and health, I had come to respect in his adversity.

My diversional hobby was becoming a force to be reckoned with in my belief system.

But even then, on that rainy Sunday, I didn't imagine the fundamental change it had already brought about, and would continue to bring about, over the years to come. From that time on there was a depth to my understanding and a new gentleness in my approach to my MS clients. I still saw their

146

frustrating traits and could discuss these with colleagues, but there was no emotional energy behind my statements of their observed behaviours, no anger at their real or exaggerated helplessness. They remained the client group I least enjoyed, but I treated them with equanimity, compassion and a deep well of patience. If, at times, my comprehension of their plight waned, always in my mind's eye I would see my other self and feel the love that surrounded him, and I would find new resources to deal with my clients.

My experience with this past life and the subsequent change in my therapeutic skills and understanding happened in the second year of my clinical work. Little did I know that I had opened my consciousness to a life story that was going to lead me to the pinnacle of my development as a therapist, lose me a year of living with the unimportant, and finally see me leave my work as a therapist, probably for ever.

I wonder if I would have embarked on the past with such a cavalier spirit if I had known? And yet I also wonder if the thread of inevitability of my life this time was not born in ancient Greece so many centuries before? Much of past-life exploration seems to be focused on unblocking blocks from the past. Perhaps it is the past that has established the foundations that allow the future to evolve.

Eighteen months ago, I was contacted by a local nursing home to visit an old client of mine whose condition had deteriorated over the past few months and needed reassessment. Emily had been one of my first clients. She had a degenerative neurological disease but was only experiencing minor problems with balance and a slight slurring of speech when tired. She had a wonderful sense of humour, was a highly educated world traveller, and wrote poetry on humourous events. She was one of those human sparklers, who I looked forward to seeing at her six-monthly reviews.

Her condition deteriorated slowly over the years, and eventually she moved into a home because physically she found living alone in a wheelchair a struggle. Her speech was difficult to understand when she was tired but otherwise was functional.

It was a different picture when the home rang me. Emily was bedridden, totally paralysed from the neck down. I was in ancient Greece again, this time living that life through another, in what was to be a most intimate, emotionally absorbing time. When I was called, Emily was expected to live a month. She lived nine.

Her speech finally deserted her completely and my constant visiting centred around spelling out the alphabet with Emily blinking her eyes (the only physical movement left to her) when I got to the right letter. Two sentences could easily take us 45 minutes. She continued to write her poetry through eye blinks, with her host of friends deciphering her intent. The humour remained.

For nine months, I drew on my own experience in ancient Greece to meet Emily's needs, at times almost telepathically. How I drew on the strength of those long-ago carers! There were times that the burden of supporting Emily and her carers, and grieving myself, was almost too much to bear. My past life in Greece allowed me to know the ultimate care to provide.

When Emily died, I grieved for myself as much as for Emily. I had lost two parts of myself. For, more than ever, I felt the collective unconscious of Jung's theory. A dead Greek, a dead Tasmanian, an alive West Australian — we were all linked. All part of some time stream that melded into an overlapping matrix.

During the nine months of Emily's care, I withdrew a great deal from the rest of my life. The time with her was so real, so human, that buying milk, listening to my friends' problems with their partners, seemed so inconsequential in comparison. It was a time of deep satisfaction for me, and heralded the end of my clinical life. Not because it had been a devastating experience. On the contrary, it had been an experience of completion.

I had achieved something special, the feeling of having done the best therapeutic work ever with no need to top it. This freed me to let go of the clinical role that had stressed me for too many years. This was a monumental decision, as all my self-worth, confidence and self-esteem were tied up in being a carer. Who would I be if I let that role go?

Five months after Emily's death, the opportunity came to create an educational role for myself, to design and implement a new service within the same organisation — a new job and a new wage! I had found my next adventure in this life.

Unlocking the events of my past life in Greece allowed me to tap into a stream of experience that rendered the events of this life more meaningful. Did I change this life with my past-life experience, or did I somehow change my life in ancient Greece by giving back what I had received? Was it my life in ancient Greece, or had I tapped into a life of another, glimpsed a memory in the stream of universal consciousness, which allowed me to fulfil known and unknown purposes now? Or did I make it all up?

Perhaps a 'yes' to this last question holds the most appeal. For if I did, then I and all the others who have 'made up' other lives, must have the most amazing capacity to balance material reality with fantasy — and with such personal magic, we can create for our world an exceptional future! However, my left brain says that the reality of past-life recall seems the most logical explanation ... doesn't it?

CAREER CHOICE

The phenomenon that our hidden emotional needs can influence our choice of career is well known: a person may choose to work in child welfare as an instinctive need to heal his or her own childhood hurts. Stella's experiences may be illustrating an extension of this, to past lives.

When we have either lived out, or consciously worked through, such an issue, events may open up for us to take another path.

SPONTANEOUS EXPLORATION

Some people encourage and persevere with continuing spontaneous recall of past lives without a guiding tape or professional assistance — as did psychiatrist Dr Arthur Guirdham and his group of fellow explorers, over several years. This is an amazing personal experience.

Yet I believe this can be doing it the hard way, because accounts of such prolonged recall tend to include severe physical accompaniments to the memories. From my experience, the recall could be finished with relatively quickly in professional sessions, with a chance that physical discomfort could be largely avoided or translated faster into improved physical wellbeing. However, some people do not realise that assistance is available. Others prefer an unassisted approach as more natural.

LEX AND BONNY'S STORY

Lex is an Englishman in his thirties, an artist who travelled widely before reaching Australia, and meeting, loving and marrying an Australian girl, Bonny. They spent six years living in a country valley in Victoria, in the coastal Otway Ranges. Lex and Bonny started a business growing organic vegetables and herbs.

The joint spontaneous past-life memories which astonished them span historical fact, personal relationships and intense mystical occurrences. Lex's description of a deeply spiritual secret initiation comes from another race.

Eighteen months after they arrived in the valley, Lex went to the State capital, Melbourne, for dental surgery. He then developed an agonising abscess in the jaw. They decided to go home and treat the abscess with natural remedies. Lex, weakened and in pain, sat on his back doorstep, grateful to be home again. Little did he know that this moment, and that pain in his head, marked the beginning of powerful spontaneous past lifetimes recall for both him and his wife, which was eventually to change the course of their lives.

LEX

Suddenly I felt I just had to lie on the ground, then I went into a trance state. I opened up my throat and out came a sound, with a vibration like a didgeridoo. I didn't consciously make it, I just heard it coming out of me. Soon tears were running down my face, I felt an incredible release — because all my life I'd needed to find this song that was particular to me, this song coming out of me, that went on for about 45 minutes. I felt great joy that I was home again.

My feeling was that I was in my long-sought-after place, I had the sense of 'a spirit of place'. Finding my song, my vibration, out of the whole world, was finding the roots of my entire being, in a timeless sort of way. I identified in a total way with the environment, but I did not consciously think then, 'I've had a past life here as an Aboriginal.'

When I was a child in England, although I had a good relationship with my family, I somehow felt a stranger in a strange land. Often when I was feeling alienated, an old black lady appeared at the end of my bed. She had an ancient feeling, I only knew she wasn't African. She was very solid, she

150

would sit on my bed, I could feel her weight and I'd have to move my legs. The feeling was, she was like a guardian angel, to remind me, of what I didn't know. I didn't know what a didgeridoo was until I recognised it on a Rolf Harris television show. Then I tried to persuade my parents to emigrate to Australia.

Bonny heard this song, came out and lay on the ground with me.

BONNY

As it went on, I lay with my head on Lex's chest, and I started feeling uneasy. I slipped into another lifetime when we were black people camping quite close. My eyes were open but I was seeing us in the surroundings as they were then, no devastation of the countryside.

I felt totally natural as a black woman, more so than I feel in my body now. This is a family camp, us and our two children. Lex (as he was) is playing a didgeridoo. I watch two or three white men creeping up, I see them give him a blow on the head. Then I have memories of me being taken prisoner and the two children killed.

By then I was getting very agitated, it was almost more real than everyday life.

LEX

When I stopped the song to help Bonny, I had a terrible pain in my head. I knew without being told that she and I were involved in a past experience of a very strong relationship. I'd wondered about this. There was a place nearby that I loved, where the river meets the sea. I'd felt it was a place of ceremonies, of power, but Bonny wouldn't go there.

BONNY

It carried sinister overtones, I didn't know why, then I found out. One day I was in trouble with my back. I'd been in bed for three days, and was also going through a pretty terrible time in my relationship with my father, who was very sick. I started hearing a weird sound, and had awful heart palpitations. Fortunately, Lex was holding me. I had a really intense past-life experience of my death in that area.

The river's course has since changed, but I was hearing the same sound of wind through the reeds. It was so strange, I was that woman running along the beach, away from my white captors. One of them shot me, in two places, including my back. I remember lying on the sand thinking, 'I know I'm dead, yet I can hear a person calling me to come back.' Then I was so shocked to find I was alive.

LEX

Bonny had slumped like a dead weight. When she relived being shot again she lurched forward. She couldn't hear me. I started yelling, 'Come back!'

BONNY

As I was dying, I recognised the man who shot me. I just knew he was my father in this life. It explained so much, my extraordinary terror of him and a deep linking with him too. We've had an odd relationship, he didn't want to share me with anyone.

After this experience, I felt relief, and an enormous sense of love and compassion for my father. Next time we visited him, I felt I was really seeing him for the first time. I understood more why he acted the way he did — and I felt I could be more of me, I was actually separating myself from him. He knew nothing about the past life, he'd have had nothing to do with such a thing.

LEX

Her father had always hated me, but that day he was very nice, it was surprising. Then he'd flip back to childhood. Then all of a sudden his eyes changed character, almost as though he'd swapped his eyes for someone else's eyes. He looked at each of us a few times and said, 'So how's the war going, then? Who's winning? Us white fellas or you black fellas?' Then he came back again, didn't know what he'd said.

Another time, I experienced my own death as the Aboriginal while a masseur was working on my neck and shoulders. I started feeling very strange, got the didgeridoo sound in my ears, and felt this blow at the back of my head. My head was really sore for a minute, then I felt a hand come across my face and a knife slit my throat. I could feel the blood dripping, felt my life draining away.

I felt quite okay about dying. I was somehow in tune with something greater than my body, while my own body was shaking — until an intense blue light flared up at the centre of my forehead.

I lost all sense of the massage room. I was a medicine man, and the most special thing to me, way beyond any life that I had, was a crystal that had been implanted in my forehead, metaphysically. In an instant, I knew everything from my memory of that lifetime. This initiation had been incredibly special, not just to that lifetime. I went through a ceremony in which the ancestors came and took me up to the sky, pulled me apart completely, cut me into pieces, then put me back together again and stitched crystals into my body.

This was good for me because all my life I'd always wanted to be more connected to magical things. I was a mystical kid, seen as different. Now I could see that that connection was natural to everyone in the Aboriginal culture.

But momentarily when I was dying I felt a tremendous fear, that I was losing the big crystal in my forehead. Afterwards I had an amazingly uplifting feeling because I realised that what was there could never be lost. I carried that initiation through even to this lifetime, and I would always have it.

The whole experience gave me more sense of purpose, a sense that I was able to get a very close transcendental connection with the land and the space all around it. And that I would have a role to play in the healing of the land, the understanding of the plants, and the spiritual forces that the land is all about. I also got interested in healing with crystals.

Bonny and I both have a feeling almost like physical immortality, that after the cow cockies who don't care about nurturing this land have left it, we will always be around it, perhaps in other bodies.

BONNY
I feel we've met one of our black children, a little white girl now, living in that area of Victoria, who's been incredibly drawn to us for all of her four years.

Further spontaneous details coming to Lex included the feeling that a white friend living near their property had also been an Aboriginal with them. A mixed group of Aboriginals had lived in the area, from different tribes, 'like refugees,' he said, 'to get away from the white man'. As an Aboriginal, the friend had seen members of a white surveying party working on setting up a lighthouse.

LEX

He'd wanted to kill these white fellas but I said no. He went off and speared one, that's why they'd come and found us. He got killed at the same time as we did.

In this life, this friend told us about places in Tasmania. So when council regulations stopped our plans and forced us out of the area we went there next, looking for land.

In deep grief at leaving their Victorian valley, Lex and Bonny crossed Bass Strait to Tasmania. Here they surprised themselves by buying a block of land near a big bay, land quite unlike what they'd thought they wanted. Bonny was drawn to it, but somehow repelled at the same time.

As they set about building a house and making a garden, the new environment triggered Bonny into deep depression. She says, 'I just had a gut feeling that something revolting had happened to me here, sometimes I just wanted to run. I had feelings of displacement, terror, alienation. I was having a lot of pain in my body, especially in my hips.'

Another spontaneous past lifetime memory, of another life shared as Aboriginals, showed Lex the crux of the new problem.

LEX

I suddenly slipped into a black person's body. I was quite old, probably in my fifties, a male. I had a sense of urgency and a bit of guilt. I was looking for somebody. I remember parting bushes near this beach and coming across a white man's campsite. I saw what I was looking for, and it was this Aboriginal girl, about 13. I got the feeling that my guilt was about this. She'd just been given to me. I didn't particularly want her, and she didn't want to be with me. She hadn't wanted to leave her own land further inland. But there was some kind of debt of honour, so neither of us could refuse. She had run away from me. This white man had captured her, tortured her, she was hanging by one leg from a tree. I felt revulsion and anger. I went running into the campsite. A shot rang out, I got a pain in my back and fell down dead.

Aboriginals were widely persecuted in both Victoria and the island State of Tasmania from the eighteenth century to earlier this century. Tasmania is infamous for the genocide of its Aboriginal population by white settlers. Lex and Bonny have found historical records supporting detail of what they felt they experienced as Aboriginals in both States.

Bonny worked through feelings about her past Tasmanian trauma for several months. She found a past lifetime practitioner and accelerated her progress with some sessions. Once the spiritual healings were complete from both her revealed lifetimes, a physical healing opportunity appeared. She found, in a nearby city, a chiropractor whose treatment of her long-standing back problem resulted in transformed posture and freedom from pain.

Her health breakthrough opened new possibilities for the couple. They decided to sell their land and expand their practices of sustainable land care and spiritual guardianship on mainland Australia.

Deep in his heart, Lex carries the feeling special to the Victorian landscape, the place that gave him his song. He says, 'I'm happy to see more of the world, but now that place will always be my place. I always go there in meditation.'

Although this spontaneous past-life recall was hard on both partners at times, it also deepened already strong bonds between them.

ADRIANA'S STORY

American social worker Kristi Jorde has written a book on the extraordinary story of her severely autistic daughter, Adriana Rocha.

Unable to communicate, the child constantly exhibited disruptive and uncontrollable behaviour. When her daughter was 9, Kristi introduced her to a keyboard technique that allows autistic people to communicate with others.

Adriana's early writing through the keyboard, with assistance, astonished her mother, who realised that the child had always been aware of what was going on around her.

Soon Adriana typed a simple message that she had been dead — and had lived other lives. Her shocked mother learned that Adriana felt she had once been a sailor, who had been angry at dying in a fire at 85 years of age, in Turkey.

Then she typed that she was autistic because she was angry.

In their book *Child of Eternity*, Kristi reports Adriana's words: that she had damaged hereself in the womb by rejecting nutrients, and so had upset her endocrine system, creating autism. Bewildered, Kristi asked how the child could know this. The 9-year-old typed that she had been educated in other lives.

SOUL WALK

Poem written to a past self of ancient Egypt

meditating on you
I lie
hands to my sides
feet together

                            did you lie so
          packed in your deathrag strips

yet rose to meet some sunrise
unsurprised
leaving your shell behind
your scarab shell
ritually fettered

                   so it could not walk again

or did you die
in the desert
with the lions

your body of that time
sundered and eaten

                      never to walk again

              now you walk in my heart
              walk without footsteps
                   walk with me
                   in my waking
                 and sleeping

friend of my soul
are you
perhaps
me?

PART THREE:

WHAT NEXT?

Chapter Ten

Changing the Past

So far we have seen in a general way how discovering the stories of past selves, and applying some personal growth techniques to them, can immediately lead to profound personal change for the better in the present self.

In this chapter, we will look more closely at other methods I use, that involve personal re-creation of new life situations. These techniques seem to allow a person to change his or her past for the better — which immediately changes something for the better in the present self's outlook, feelings, attitudes and perhaps even body.

The first group of 'Change the Past' processes involves imagining with intent. They are used around death, to facilitate a present self to let go of a past self.

The second process, which I call 'Gift from the Future', enables the traveller to access profound tools for change from deeper in consciousness. This facilitates spontaneous re-creation of an improved life story.

Both techniques require openness and an impeccable approach to facing deep truth, by both practitioner and client. While teaching the techniques is beyond the function of this book, I can discuss them and show some effects.

At first, the idea of changing the past may seem unthinkable. Our society has not prepared us for this. There lies the past, set in concrete. Some people are so attached to this view that they will vigorously defend their God-given right to illness and unhappiness which seemingly stems from the past. They do indeed have that right.

Nor has our conditioning prepared us to deal with the concept that we create our own reality. Life just happens to us, doesn't it?

But becoming conscious, or aware, allows us to specifically understand how we have created, or attracted, our present-life situations, both knowingly and unknowingly. Once we're aware, we have the right to improve on our creations.

Here I'll review a point previously stated: the past is not dead and gone until we have finished with it. Psychologists agree that traces of the past of this life are active and visible in our present feelings, attitudes, thoughts, conversations and behaviour. Psychological problems rooted in the past remain alive in the present until we resolve old issues, or wear them out over years. The same seems true for issues that apparently begin during our distant lives.

HOW THE PAST IS ALIVE
An example illustrates how the past can be alive in the present. A 40-year-old man repeatedly eats all the food on his plate whether or not his body wants it, because 'my mother always taught me not to waste food'. To bring his awareness into the present moment, the question could be, 'Why do you so often choose to stuff your body with food it may not need?'

From old habit we move on to more serious issues. Perhaps someone is carrying a burden of poor self-image or illness aggravated, or even caused by, emotional blockages or physical trauma stemming from someone else's life, at some other time — a past life. An event or set of circumstances in the current life triggers the problem, even as far back as birth, with reinforcing situations in later life.

We may approach the problem through seeing influence from relevant past lifetimes as either metaphor, or direct cause.

PAST LIVES AS METAPHOR
Past lives as a liberating tool in their aspect of metaphor allow easy access to present-day, unfinished emotional issues, in the guise of other situations involving past selves and the people with whom they interacted.

For example, a man wanting to know the cause of his constant feelings of anger discovers three past lives in which he was brutally imprisoned and physically crippled, with no opportunity to state his case. As he works to resolve these similar past life situations, he is strengthened to face a situation of imposed constriction and hurt from his earlier years in the present life; this is likely to be preceded by anger at being constricted, hurt, and unable to speak out during birth. By the time he starts to deal with present-life issues, some of the anger will have dissolved.

PAST LIVES AS DIRECT CAUSE
Sometimes a present crisis seems to stem directly from past life

memory, compared with which its present-life triggers are minor. The baffling mind/body disease of *anorexia nervosa* might be a case in point. An eating disorder that can waste a usually young body to death, it is known to happen to some girls who in childhood had low self-esteem and were over-conscientious.

Dr Woolger has suggested that *anorexia nervosa* could originate in unfinished business in the past — that it expresses unconsciously held trauma from starvation in previous lives, caused by famine, disease, or war. He refers to numbers of stories of starvation in World War 11 concentration camps emerging from the unconscious minds of contemporary sufferers from *anorexia nervosa*, who had no connection with such conditions and were born after the war. He also speculates that colic in babies and other eating disorders may have similar origins.

The stories comprising past-life-as-metaphor or past-life-as-direct-cause may both be historically true. In both cases I have used the following 'Change the Past' techniques with success.

1. Imaginative 'Change the Past' technique
This is applied around death, to facilitate the letting go of a past self's persona.

Do you remember dying? Death is experienced in past-life work as an altered state of consciousness. Countless people recalling past lifetimes have recalled the deaths that concluded those lives. Those deaths may have been peaceful, violent, expected or sudden.

Remembering a past death is a unique experience, and it can quickly dissolve terror about death. Someone who has spent a lifetime fearing death can feel fear fall away after recalling a past self's death. This suggests great potential for past-life work as spiritual healing with people facing death from illness or age.

Usually I advise travellers to 'move through the death and tell me what you're experiencing'. If the dying is painful, I suggest they move through it quickly, rather than avoid it, because there is more practical benefit in experiencing. Only if the death is horrific do I invite the traveller to skip ahead to after death. Then we may later carefully revisit the crisis to heal its charge.

(a) *'Thank you, body, and good-bye' technique.* Now I directly involve the traveller's creative imagination. I find it valuable to have the spirit of the past self 'see' and 'stroke' his or her dead body, thank it for allowing Earth experience, and say goodbye to it before moving on. This is a completion process at the physical level of consciousness. (I assume this is changing the past! I have no infallible source on whether this happens naturally.)

(b) *'Completing with the body' technique.* Then, spontaneously, or at my suggestion, instead of drifting off after death, the traveller may accelerate time to view what happened to the body whose spirit has left, to watch the funeral if there is one, as it actually happened. (When this happens automatically in the regression, we wonder if that spirit really was there.)

Being present at a past self's funeral can be a rich experience for the time traveller. New realisations can emerge, as, say, the past self hears comments from people present, or receives insight into mourners' true feelings. The self may try to communicate with them, express regret, sorrow or love, although there is usually a feeling of detachment. In one case, a spirit watched her own embalming, finally accepting the love of the friend performing it.

Many times, the traveller finds a body is left to rot or to be savaged by animals. Once this situation is acknowledged and felt, I may ask a traveller if he or she would like to recreate an ideal funeral to honour that body. Usually the answer is yes, and the result a powerful and moving completion of an unfinished situation. Especially when the past self had been lonely or anguished, this is an opportunity for the present self to express loving care to himself or herself, by proxy.

Now, in imagination, the traveller may compose the body, reassemble a severed body or charred remains, restore a damaged body — clean it, clothe it in beautiful robes, and place it perhaps in an ornate coffin in the ground. Or he or she may carry out neglected funeral rites of that culture, perhaps wrapping the body in bark and placing it in a tree. A Viking may need a coin placed in his mouth and the body sent to sea in his burning ship. Someone else may inter a body simply, in a beautiful place in Nature well loved by that past self, surrounded by forest animals that had been friends. Both the traveller and I are likely to be moved to tears by the beauty of the fantasised ritual.

This process can involve spiritual or transpersonal elements such as tunnels, celestial light, and spiritual figures.

By consciously changing the fully acknowledged past in this manner, the individual creates an old situation anew, out of overview. This kind of letting go of the old can be a step in releasing unwanted bleed-through from connected past lifetime problems.

Sometimes it seems as though these processes connect us with ghosts. As I guided a woman to release her vengeful past self from haunting her parents in France, even long after they were dead,we wondered if we were actually terminating sounds of ghostly chains in some old French building.

2. The 'Gift from the Future' process

This technique moves past the intent to imagine. Once a past lifetime of suffering has been fully dealt with, the future self — that is, the time traveller — is enabled to empower the past self to re-create or relive his or her life story again, quickly and vividly, in easier ways. In other words, the present self evolves the past self to a higher state of life mastery.

Consciousness research studies have shown that the mind does not know the difference between a real memory and an event vividly perceived through inner senses. In this second process, the traveller's deeper mind is encouraged to both generate and adopt a better reality, from a more powerful and evolved viewpoint. Results seem almost alchemical.

Simply imagining a wretched life improved does not achieve lasting results. To be effective, this technique must involve a more profound layer of consciousness. It is not reprogramming by repeated suggestion, which would leave the underlying origin of misery or disaster intact. Nor is it a hypnotic technique where the unconscious mind is directed to heal the cause.

I first came across this technique in a basic form through an international past lifetimes therapist, several years ago. As I have worked with it since, it has revealed its own rules. It can be applied only in cases where the past individual could reasonably take advantage of new opportunity — provided by the traveller — to make new choices. Choices cannot be made for other people in the life story. And the technique is not applicable where the past 'aggressor' was massive social change, for example, large-scale war.

165

To illustrate the 'Gift from the Future' process, here is an account of two sessions with an attractive young woman who aimed to resolve a number of problems.

Case study: Anorexia

Ten years previously, Claire had survived anorexia and bulimia. Now she felt symptoms returning strongly, such as overeating yet not being able to judge when her stomach was full. She also complained of emotions stuck in her body ('feelings of death, in my stomach'), of holding back from her femininity, of spiritual blockage, and of lack of trust in her male partner.

During our initial interview Claire volunteered a number of items, each of which could have provided a session target of 'the past lifetime where this began'. As a child she had suffered mysterious recurring stomach pains. Confessing to hating the sound of argument, she said, 'Raised voices destroy me.' In a number of accidents she had suffered injuries to her face and head. However, she now chose a larger goal: 'the past lifetime most blocking me now'.

First session

Claire's first impression is of many people talking in a marketplace, of horses and carts, smells of cooking and herbs. She is a young olive-skinned girl with fair hair, wearing a brown tunic and skin shoes tied at the ankle. She says, 'This is a place I know, but I feel wild, I don't trust anyone.' The girl's name is Helena, it is a Middle Eastern country in the sixteenth century.

Helena mourns her previous home in a country area, where until recently she had lived with her mother, young brother and father. As she mentions her father, tears spill over her face.

Regression: He used to pick me up and hug me, talk to me, hold my hand. But he went on a journey. Robbers killed him.

Now we're on a donkey cart, moving to a town. It's scary, so many people! Another man lives with us now. I don't like him. I'm about 15, a virgin. He rapes me. More than once.

My mother's sick, very frail, I wish I could help her, I'd like to trust her. I think he's poisoning her. Now she's died, taken away on a cart. He doesn't seem to care. All the furniture goes.

I'm sitting in the sun, someone brushes my hair. It's an older market lady with a lovely face.

166

Now I'm 18. I live in a big place with lots of other girls on the side of a mountain above the town. It's a religious place. He sold me to it! I'm angry, but I feel good too, I'm safe.

This is a very strict place. We have some food, broth, occasionally meat, but a lot of the time we're hungry. Our bodies need to be thin, we're all being prepared for a ceremony. That's exciting but I feel fearful too.

There's a lot of laughter. My clothes are beautiful, we all wear white. I spend time with other girls in the sun. We learn about herbs from older women, they don't need to be thin. They lock us in at night.

Now it's time for the ceremony. We form two lines in our white dresses, we walk up wide stairs with our candles. ('I've seen this procession before! In dreams !')

We go into a big round room. The older women take us to our places, we stand in a circle facing men.

Everyone's scared! Some girls try to run away. We're going to die! It's for the god. It wasn't meant to be like this! My hands are being tied, my friends are screaming, there are knives and blood.

They cut out my stomach.

There's blood everywhere, the girls are all dead. The men are chanting loudly, they don't care, they've got our insides on trays above their heads, walking around chanting. They're offering our insides to the god for fertility...

Claire and I work to clear some of the trauma from this story, which encompasses a number of elements of her current concerns: emotions around fear of death 'stuck in my stomach', holding back from the femininity that led to Helena being raped and later killed; distrust of a man; connections with food and being thin; and the notion that 'raised voices destroy me'.

Using a 'Change the Past' technique, Claire visualises that Helena's spirit rescues her tortured body, returns its entrails and ritually buries it in a field of flowers in the presence of angels.

When Helena's spirit reaches a higher dimension, more information arrives. Her rapist also had her father killed, in a conspiracy with her mother, before he tired of her mother. Helena begins to work through rage and hate with this man — whom Claire recognises as a man she knows now — as well

167

as grief around abandonment from her father's dying. At the end of the session she is still crying, but beginning to feel better.

Second session
Because Claire then moved to a country area, she did not return for a follow-up session for four months. Then she reported she'd had a healing crisis after the first session, with feelings of hopelessness and an upsurge in early anorexia symptoms. She said she had dealt with this by spending time in Nature. She had been amazed that on the weekend following her discovery of this story, the man she felt had been Helena's rapist had visited mutual friends in Claire's new town. She still felt distrust of him.

Although I urged her to continue healing Helena's life, Claire preferred to focus on current issues of a relationship crisis, and a pattern of accidents to her face and head.

As we work with a quick-release breath technique, Claire quickly achieves a shift on fears around the relationship. I then apply a body-response technique to find ultimate, metaphysical causes of the accident pattern. Five causes emerge, two in Claire's lifetime, which we attend to, and three in past lives. Two of the three past-life causes occur in Helena's story.

Claire picks up Helena's story again easily, at a time when she has been at the religious establishment for seven months. She feels that the style of worship involves the sun and several gods, one with a human body and an animal head. More detail emerges.

Regression: *I'm watching a very beautiful marriage between people who are like our king and queen in this place. I'd like this to happen to me.*

Later there's lots of unrest, the new queen is not bearing a child. The king's upset. It's like a curse — other people will be infertile too. Lots of people give gifts of fruit and plants to the king and queen.

Now there's a ceremony for the queen, with the magical woman and one man, our religious head. Oils and candles burning, chanting and dancing around her, splashing potions on her. I'm watching. (Claire winces.) I think the queen's dead! Oh! They disembowelled her, for infertility.

Now I'm being killed the same way.

168

We release more charge from the death trauma. Then I direct her to find the causes in Helena's life of the chain of accidents to Claire's face and head.

Regression: I'm in my room at the religious place. A lady who teaches me comes in. She needs to cut my face. I must have two scars high on both cheeks. Some others have this. I'm afraid. It's an initiation, it has to be done. Deep down I don't believe that, it's to make sure I stay there.

She uses a fine blade. It hurts more emotionally. (She weeps in grief.) *They're taking away the beauty I've just found.*

Now it's another time. I'm becoming of high esteem, another initation. They cut me around the eyes. ('The accidents cut around my eyes!') *I'm begging someone to stop something, for myself and others. Oh, they're telling me I have to do this work now.*

I'm crying. I want to die. I have no control over my life.

Directed to the second ultimate cause of the accidents pattern, Claire finds herself back in Helena's mother's house.

Regression: My mother's boyfriend's there, trying to make love to me. No. I hate him. He's grabbed my hair, holding a torch (fire) to my face. He rapes me.

I was a virgin and it hurt. He says, "I own you." It's not true.

After we deal with trauma release from these events, I employ the 'Gift from the Future' technique.

Claire is deeply relaxed. I ask her how Helena's character makeup might have contributed to the tragic end of her life. We discuss this, and Claire decides she wants to bestow Helena with a particular spiritual quality she feels able to impart. In visualisation she does this, and the past self accepts it.

Now I guide Helena to quickly report her life again. We find that as a seven-year-old, Helena sulks in 'my special place', resentful of a new baby brother. And after the move to the city, Helena realises her mother has become a prostitute to make money. One night she sees her mother crying and bruised, but feels 'disrespect'.

As a street child, Helena makes friends with a kind woman who sells herbs at a market stall. Now the story begins to change, as the effects of Claire's gift emerge. Helena at the age of 19 attends a ceremony in a house where she now lives with a group of women herbalists, friends of her market friend. She reports excitedly, 'I've learned a lot. I make herbal mixtures.' Returning to her first meeting with these women, Helena says, 'I desperately wanted to change my environment. They offered to teach me. I went with them. It feels GREAT!'

(Claire whispers to me, 'Why has it all changed?' I ask, 'Do you want to go on with it?' She says, 'Yes!')

Exploration of the new version of the life is done extremely quickly. Yet emotions are still experienced in depth. Helena next meets a prosperous male healer, they fall in love, marry, work together and have four children. At the age of 48, after reviewing her many years of happiness with gratitude, the new version of Helena dies peacefully in her bed. Claire does not ('yet') know this man.

Claire is ecstatic and astonished. 'I feel so different,' she says. A month later she tells me, 'Since that session I've felt fantastic.' The problems are dissolving, although she may have further work to do. A year later she has lost *anorexia nervosa* symptoms that had recurred all through her life.

Case study: a knee problem
Our second example of 'Gift from the Future' concerns Catherine, a health practitioner attending a past lifetime training course. About the time she enrolled for the course, some months earlier, she had become aware of pain in her left knee. When it persisted she sought medical attention but a doctor found nothing diagnosable. She continued to feel pain. I asked her if she would like to explore the metaphysical causes. Intrigued, she agreed.

First session
I guide her to 'the past life where this problem began'. She feels she is Joan, a countrywoman in England in the last century. A few years after her marriage, Joan feels discontented and angry about lack of communication between herself and her husband. But as she has been taught not to express unpleasant feelings, she says nothing.

One day, after driving her young daughter to school, Joan turns the horse and cart homeward. A storm comes up. Lightning frightens the horse which rears, flinging her on to the road. The heavy cart runs over her left leg at the knee. Dazed, helpless and bleeding, she lies face down in mud in the rain until her husband finds her some hours later.

At home in bed, Joan is losing blood fast. She hears the doctor tell her husband that the only way to save her life would be to amputate the leg, but even that may not be enough. Shocked, her husband at first refuses. When later he reluctantly assents, the operation is performed. Joan dies.

Catherine was powerfully moved by this story. Her own left knee was throbbing. As we worked with this material, she was startled to recognise Joan's husband as her own first husband — who in this life had had a foot amputated. We speculated on whether, if this story were true, unconscious guilt about his decision on Joan's fatal amputation might have attracted a similar situation to himself now.

We also looked at the proposition that perhaps all accidents are ultimately caused by hidden anger. Joan had been angrily brooding for years about her relationship.

Second session

Next day we returned to Joan's story. After Catherine reconnects with Joan's feelings and circumstances, I suggest she find and share with Joan a particular spiritual quality she chooses from a deep level of consciousness.

Catherine now quickly lives out a new version of Joan's life. This Joan has both better skills in communication, which she uses within her marriage, and more opennness to other points of view. She is not angry about her relationship, but delights in it.

Joan continues to drive her daughter safely to school until she has another baby. Catherine reports Joan's increasing domestic enjoyment and the arrival of two more babies. Joan Two lives a long rewarding life with her husband and four children, and finally dies peacefully.

Afterwards Catherine, smiling out of Joan's happiness, said: 'But I kept waiting for the accident!' I pointed out that her gift to Joan had obviated Joan's need to feel and suppress anger. In this case, no anger meant no accident.

Throughout the course, Catherine's knee quickly returned to normal. A year later there has been no recurrence of the pain.

PLAYING WITH TIME

In playing with time in past-life work, we speak of 'going back to past lives,' to re-experience them. This, of course, is not true. Past-life work invites the memory into our present moment. We deal with its material in the present moment. Change for the better occurs in the present moment, through the medium of the other-life story.

Playing around with time through the 'Change the Past' processes I am describing really means changing our perception of the past. With the 'Gift from the Future', the traveller is not aware that his or her perception is altering until change has been reported. Both create improvement travellers achieve themselves, through their own choices and actions in the present.

An observer might wonder, where does that original past-life story 'go'? According to time travellers who have experienced this process, the original story seems to dissolve, even though they can easily remember what first happened if they want to. But something deep has shifted, and the shift has present consequences.

During regression, the traveller's time sense is altered. We witness an acceleration effect, therefore shifts of energy are achieved relatively quickly. In regression, one can sense time telescoping and looping. This brings us closer to the quantum physics concept that all time actually occurs simultaneously. As such amazing concepts enter mass consciousness, these days I am often asked, 'But if everything is happening now, how can past lives exist?'

Because our physical self senses time as linear, the simultaneous time hypothesis can be hard to grasp. How could all our lifetimes possibly be happening at once? Can we exist in many time-frames and locations at once? Such profound questions about the nature of consciousness and the material universe are addressed by new physicist Dr David Bohm, who propounds the theory that matter and consciousness are an unbroken whole.

But in everyday terms, perhaps the greatest challenge in the concept of simultaneous time is the effect it has on our favourite explanation for events: cause and effect. If we let go of this model, would we then have to look at some tricky questions? Would it mean that we are actually making all our choices in the present moment — to be unhappy, ill and constricted, or happy, healthy and free? What would happen to our reasons? Our excuses? 'I'm this way because my parents were horrible to me.' And they may have been.

Well, if all time were happening at once, in each moment we would clearly see where the impetus comes from, but the choices we make in each moment would be our own present responsibility. Tremendous personal power resides in becoming conscious in the moment.

In past-life work we are not limited by linear time. In regression we are free to dart about in time. And life issues connect through association, rather than through time logic. Our most recent past life is not necessarily the one with the most influence on us now.

Case study: back damage

An example of how layers of old pain from centuries back may combine into a major body ailment comes from Sally. During an intensive two-year personal growth journey, she integrated the 'Gift from the Future' process as one element in a quest to improve her health and quality of life.

Sally's story begins with the birth of her first baby, which led to chronic lower-back pain. X-rays showed a minor congenital defect which led to spondylitis (inflammation of the joints of the backbone).

Sally says: 'After seven years and another baby I found I could no longer cope on five hours of broken sleep with large doses of painkillers and sleeping tablets. The option I was given then was to continue to survive on drugs, with the possibility of kidney damage in later life, or surgery.

'Eventually, in a five-hour operation I had a spinal fusion, where bone was cut from my hips and grafted over the fourth lumbar vertebra. Although the operation was a success, it took me many years to recover from the surgery, and I was left with a large numb area, about 20 centimetres square, and a deep internal ache. On the first day of my period the pain was often close to intolerable. I also developed a chronic stiff neck.

'Seventeen years later, I started rebirthing sessions to help with emotional stress. In many of these I had spontaneous recall of past lifetimes where there was back and neck trauma — being shot, spiked, beheaded, speared and kicked in the

173

spine by jackboots. Much of the neck pain cleared as I relived my own birth, discovering that I was a facial presentation baby, born with my head back. I was releasing that cellular memory of pain.

'In a past-life regression I visited the most significant past life concerning my back pain. As Dariel, a youth in ancient Greece, I left home after an argument with my father. A group of bandits kidnapped me for ransom and brutally kicked me to death. I felt my father had betrayed me because he had not paid the ransom and rescued me. I felt I could not trust men.'

In another session, Sally gifted Dariel spiritually. He was then able to outwit the bandits — and to realise that his father had not received the ransom note. She says, 'Since then I have not experienced any period pain in my spine.'

She also found that she had spent several past lifetimes as a spastic. She says: 'These people live in bodies with permanent muscular stress. Once I was a spastic child of 12, Marnie, living with my mother in abject poverty. When my mother died I was left alone, and I died of starvation, strapped in my wheelchair.

'Louise Hay says that back pain is a result of feeling unsupported. For spastic people to survive they need some physical support. Marnie died without it. I had the spinal fusion when I was 28, at a time I felt unsupported. My partner worked nightshift and I was caring for two small boys.

'In rebirthing, I discovered that my own mother had temporarily left me soon after my birth. I'd felt overwhelmingly betrayed. I'd decided never to trust anyone again.

'In another regression, I was a barrow boy in London last century, living off my wits. I was caught picking a pocket and transported to Australia but I died in transit.'

Following through on the central feeling of being unsupported — emotionally, and also literally, as the back supports the body — Sally allowed the pickpocket to recreate his life. He chose to build up a support group to keep a look-out.

She said, 'From this, I set about creating a group of friends around me now — then at first refused to allow myself to be supported by them because I didn't trust them! But I now am accepting support.'

Recently, Sally rebirthed again on the back pain. She sobbed for a long time when she found that she had decided God had not supported her over many centuries.

During all this growth work, Sally's back gradually improved. But she felt there was more. As a culmination, a further breath session cleared foggy feelings of anaesthetic from the back operation. She describes the sensation: 'As I continued to breathe I felt tingling creep down my legs and up my spine. Another miracle was happening! I began to feel heat burning right through that numb area, I could actually feel my hands touching it! My back glowed all night long, and by next morning the entire area was warm and pink. At last I was able to feel supported! I'm really grateful to all my helpers, including my past selves.'

Such material change gives us clues to the mechanisms of human reality creation — where each one of us is an explorer. As we change something in our consciousness for the better, so our reality adjusts.

Chapter Eleven

The Unexplained

Past-life work puts us in touch with aspects of ourselves that were previously hidden by the mechanistic world view of the modern era, that says we are each only a biological machine whose boundary is our skin.

It is no coincidence that the upsurge of interest in past-life exploration is happening in the century when science is revealing revolutionary new dimensions of reality, that were previously blocked out by this mechanistic world view and value system. The mechanistic outlook has dominated our culture for 300 years. It is called the Newtonian-Cartesian world view because it derived from the convictions of scientist Isaac Newton and philosopher Rénè Dèscartes — that all reality can be analysed for scientific certainty. New discoveries show that as a world view this position is now obsolete, because it is not the whole picture of reality. It is only a segment.

To entertain the possibility of past lifetimes is to take part in a global shift in consciousness which began in the 1920s with the emergence of Einsteinian physics and quantum physics, both of which challenge accepted ideas of the laws of nature and consciousness. In the last 20 years the new ideas have gained momentum in mass awareness.

Modern science now juggles with unimaginable concepts. For example, possibilities that consciousness can exist in matter are showing up not only in modern physics but also in biology, information and systems theory and thermodynamics. Accepted boundaries of matter, consciousness, time, space and even identity are being vitally challenged in many ways. Reality is not what we thought. We are having to learn new ways of looking at life.

Such a shift in perception is required when we consider the following concepts as they begin to come to public attention.

PAST LIVES AS ANIMALS?

Regression: I have an ape-like body, crouched, daytime. A clearing on the edge of jungle. It's not safe! I don't know whether to run or stay. (This young man, George, trembles.) *I've seen so many of my kind die, by lions, tigers, vicious animals. I'm furry, long fur, big toes — three other toes not so well formed. Hands have fur on the back, the skin is white. The fur is black-brown, lighter on the ends of the fingers and toes. My head is round and flat, baldish. My face is narrowish, eyes close together, flat nose. I'm humanoid.*

I like to eat soft fruit and drink milk from coconuts I break by throwing them on rocks so the milk does not spill away. Now I'm clubbing a lion to death. Something strange. I feel a huge urge to eat some of its raw flesh. I haven't eaten animal flesh before.

My kind spend most of our days in treetops, to get away from gangs of people with crude weapons. We try to protect ourselves with rough spears for stabbing. Now I'm invited into a village for a feast of cooked meat, prepared by taller people whose spears have stone points. I like the cooked meat.

But the smell of cooking attracts humanoid attackers. (George trembles again, his voice rises.) *They have better weapons, things they can propel big rocks by, and spears... Oh, I see! We never thought to throw our spears, we just stick them into things. Theirs are made better, when they throw them they stay on course.*

Before he can experiment with these new weapons, he dies by one of them.

A woman describes this past self:

Regression: *I'm trying to stand up. It's very difficult. I can only do it for a short time. I'm more comfortable on all fours. I'm an ape. I really enjoy climbing up trees and swinging, it's really fun. I eat sweet fruits, lots of them. I have pinky skin. My eyes look very alive, dark brown and moist. I'm a male. The thing I do best is eat.*

('Why do you want to stand?') *It feels very tall. I can see so much better. It's not easy. I want to be taller than everyone else. I'm bigger this way. I break branches off trees. But I can't walk. I take a few steps and I fall forward.*

How can humans recall being animals? And did such creatures as these ever exist? Possibly, they did. The latest news from scientists studying human fossils is that five to eight million years ago, humans and chimpanzees actually did diverge from a common ancestor.

True stories or not, at the personal level these travellers gave themselves strong metaphors. Did the nervous 'humanoid' need the adrenalin rush his fear produced to spur him into making some major move in this life? Was the woman attempting for the first time in her life to stand up for herself in some way?

Dr Morris Netherton is one of a number of past lifetime therapists who report that people's accounts of their first life on Earth are often of animals. One of the animals in my story file resembles a dinosaur, which could have been on Earth as long ago as one hundred million years.

My clients have also experienced 'being' birds and insects. Some of these lives are fleeting. Occasionally such a story can discharge masses of emotion, usually fear, as did an account of a praying mantis captured by flying creatures and immobilised, awaiting being eaten.

This is an instance of how past-life exploration expands understanding and compassion from within, not only for other people — making prejudice hard to sustain — but for any creature we temporarily identify with. Our consciousness is not even confined to Earth life, but seems able to range to other worlds and dimensions of existence.

DEATH AND BEYOND

Travellers' experiences around death, and beyond, report much that cannot be explained by contemporary convention — such as continuing to exist after experiencing death. Past deaths are sometimes accompanied by terror and pain, but many people report feeling relief at dying, and some feel even mystical exaltation.

A traveller, Donna, was not expecting death for the past self she discovered strolling on a hot morning in ancient Egypt among flowers massed in an enormous garden. 'Wonderful perfumes, they're overpowering,' says Donna, weeping with joy and nostalgia. (Today Donna is an aromatherapist.)

Regression: I'm walking, wearing a thin long dress. I feel sad. I'm the servant girl of a young priestess. Is she dead? Another handmaiden and I have to go with her. Oh. We're going to her tomb. Oh ...

I have to go. I don't want to.

They're doing ceremonies. I'm very frightened. I have to do this, I've been trained for it, it's a great honour. Now they've sealed the door. I think she's dead, she's in a sort of coffin. It's getting hot in here. I feel terrified.

She describes her feelings in the ensuing hours or days, ritually entombed: panic and horror meshing with feelings of sacred duty. The two girls fight to breathe, to stay conscious, attempting continual prayer to their gods. I ask, 'What will happen to you if you die?' She says confidently, 'The wings will come for me.' She describes the ancient Egyptian symbol of the winged disc.

Time drags on. The tomb gets hotter, the girls weaker. 'The wings will come, they will come! The other girl's resting against the coffin, we're losing consciousness.' A long time later she says, 'I hear them — the wings! I see the winged disc above me! It's rushing towards me. I'm transfixed. Oh — I see it sideways — it's not a disc, it's a spiral.

'All I can hear is a whooshing sound.' Then silence.

Coming back slowly to awareness of the consulting room, Donna is speechless. She feels she has touched the divine. Was it death, or mystical initiation? Donna did not then know that for centuries in ancient and tribal cultures, the spiral has symbolised the progress of the soul towards eternal life.

Later Donna wrote, 'I did not go through a death as such, but a ritual initiation. It was an incredible experience of being lifted into a spiral emanating from a disc on wings, which sprang back on itself and out the other side, into a different dimension.

'The lesson is so profound. I had been entombed in my own negative beliefs, I am now spiritually free to go ahead.'

Donna has since opened a training centre for alternative therapists.

The mysteries of death — and of life — enthral us. There is so much we do not understand.

CHANGES IN 'THE LIGHT'

In exploring the validity of non-ordinary experience, transper-

179

sonal counselling often requires that we move into the unknown. As Australian psychologist Dr Cherie Sutherland reports in her book *Transformed by the Light*, one of the most common experiences of people who have been near death, but have returned to life, is to see and enter a realm of light whose characteristics are so unfamiliar that they struggle to describe it and its ineffable effects on them.

When travellers report this experience, I take it seriously. But more than that — in utilising natural phenomena from changing states of consciousness, especially from near-death experiences, in past-life work I find the after-death state of celestial light a fruitful realm for practical healing work .

Back in 1983, a Gallup Poll in the U.S. revealed that eight million people had some mystical experience through having clinically died and returned to life, or having almost died. In the last 30 years, escalating studies worldwide of the near-death experience by medical and psychological researchers, and by those who have experienced this state, have recorded the phenomenon extensively.

Travellers who move through awarenesses of past deaths find they have easy access to visualising this light. In doing so, they seem to bring powerful spiritual energies to bear on their mundane affairs. While the spirit of the past self moves blissfully through the light, I may invite first a graphic release of emotional burdens brought through from the past-life story.

As the traveller experiences the light as a safe and intensely personal territory of consciousness, the past self's spirit is in an ideal situation to finish major emotional business with any characters from the life who still hold a charge. On this ethereal 'stage', even turbulent emotions can be safely played out as steps on the way to understanding, forgiveness, new peace and a greater capacity for love.

A bonus is that some of the important characters in such a story have possibly been identified by the traveller as characters in present or former relationships in the current life story. Insight and increased understanding happen almost instantaneously through processing, and are then taken out into the present relationships. (However, I caution people to stay responsible for their own perceptions. It is unwise to announce to husband or wife, 'You cheated on me in a past life!' If sharing is appropriate, it is more truthful to say, 'I understand my feelings better now and I've worked through some of them today.')

In the light, without hypnosis, often with high emotion and spiritual intuitions, the traveller balancing on the edge of active imagination can find himself or herself 'being': the past self's spirit; either the present or past self interacting with spiritual guides or teachers; the past self remembering physical life with other people, at any age; the present self interacting with the past self ('we've become great friends,' said a traveller); the present or past self interacting with loved ones from the present life who have died, whether adult, child or foetus; or a future self.

Just why this light is such an effective healing territory for present or past selves cannot be fully explained.

Meanwhile, when we re-experience a past death, we approach the high spiritual purpose of dying consciously — just as people re-experiencing their own birth approach conscious birthing, just as those re-experiencing a past lifetime approach more conscious living now. Being born, living, dying — the dance of the ages — sweeps us all into constant play.

NEW PERSPECTIVES

In *The Holotropic Mind,* Dr Stanislav Grof states that acceptance of the transpersonal nature of consciousness radically challenges many beliefs we take for granted. It means to accept that our lives are affected not only by what happens in our immediate environment from birth to death, but also by a host of intangible influences, including spiritual, and even cosmic.

It is currently inexplicable that we may, apparently, experience intimately the deaths, as well as the lives, of other human beings — that we can perhaps channel the essence of other people through our own biological equipment. As units of universal energy, our thoughts may be viewed as electrical energy, our emotions as magnetic energy, the matter of our bodies as energy vibrating at a slower frequency that makes it appear solid to our senses. Our make-up seems to include unknown energies just beginning to be detected by instruments of modern science.

The complex unit that constitutes every human individual is apparently separate from all other such units, and from everything else on the planet. Yet according to new physicist Dr David Bohm, nothing in science supports separatism, it is an illusion. Even the sharp edges of a block of wood seen microscopically resemble edges of clouds. So do all other apparent edges.

Einstein has told us that we live in a universe from which no energy is lost and to which no energy is added. We are components of this universal system. On a planet estimated to be four and a half billion years old, the atoms of our present physical forms will have existed in objects and other living beings ranging from oceans to wombats — and possibly even in stars.

The sages insist, 'We are all One.'

ASTROLOGICAL OVERVIEW

Astrology is a study that sees Earth and human life as components of a universe in constant energetic play. It claims that energy events we see having a physical impact on the universe above are also having an impact on our consciousness — and have been, throughout all the lives we may have lived. It is not so much that the stars influence us, it is that we and the stars are all taking part in a great theatre of action.

Astrologists say that our planet has recently moved out of the astrological Earth Age ruled by the sign of Pisces, a 2000-year cycle beginning around the birth of Jesus Christ and ending in the second half of this century. Piscean characteristics demonstrate duality. For example, in a global sense, patriarchy, authority-oriented religion and monarchy are now widely seen as divisive institutions fostering a them-and-us outlook, currently breaking down. The Piscean emphasis on personal sacrifice no longer, in the 'nineties, has such an honored place. At a new edge of social outlook, polarised attitudes of spirituality versus sexuality, winner versus loser, and so on, are beginning to dissolve, although they remain apparent in many past-life stories.

In this view, the burgeoning energies of the Aquarian Age are humanity's natural dynamic for the next 2000 years. Some Aquarian attributes are equality, unity, and self-responsibility. This 'New Age' is not just the 'Old Age' in a new dress, although this is a comfortable interpretation. The two major eras differ radically on fundamental values and behaviour, as we see by lifestyle and political changes that have been occurring on a global scale over recent years.

For example, the Piscean trait of following orders has given way to a marked trend to seek the expert within oneself, an Aquarian trait. This has led to the upsurge of citizens' groups that challenge formerly entrenched authorities, such as government, law and church. Former concepts of patriotism, nationalism, and blind allegiance are being eroded. 'My country, right or wrong' is for many people outdated, government is no longer assumed to be right, nor necessarily benevolent, as it is for many past selves encountered, say, around both World Wars.

Broad signs of the disintegration of Piscean Age issues of separation lie in the environment protection movement as it has gathered strength from all strata of society, Gorbachev's episode of *glasnost*, the sudden dismantling of the Berlin Wall, the amount of publicised attention given to the rights of racial minorities including Australian Aboriginals, and to the rights of not only women but also children and animals. In the West, the drive towards self-responsibility has created the rapidly expanding movement which teaches how to achieve personal growth individually and collectively.

The human race is still experiencing the cusp, or transition stage, between eras where major attitudes overlap confusingly. We may cling to the old. But in a survey of the changeover, astrologer Marion Weinstein has pointed out that ultimately there is no real choice: the old order yields to the new, as Alfred Lord Tennyson observed in a poem, adding, 'And God fulfills himself in many ways.'

It is as self-defeating to adhere to tenets of a former Age as it would be to cling to the persona of a past self. To live in the moment we need to honour the paramount values of both this present age and this present lifetime.

AWAKENING ABILITIES OF THE PSYCHE

Many sources claim that one of the characteristics of the birthing Age of Aquarius is the awakening in humans of the awareness of more than five senses, an awareness of subtle psychic senses that have lain dormant in the majority of people up to now. Futurists such as psychologist Dr Jean Houston presume these abilities to be emerging because humanity will need them for survival in coming centuries.

Recall of past lifetimes can be viewed as a psychic activity even for people who see themselves as non-psychic. It can be seen as an expression of clairvoyance, clairaudience or clairsentience — inner seeing, hearing, sensing — available relatively easily.

Apart from the blending with past selves, some apparently psychic experiences reported to me in session include telepathic communication with animals, babies, foetuses, ghosts, leprechauns and people who have died; a re-living of the birth and death of a brother who died before the traveller was born; memories of a dead father's traumatic accident experienced by a present self who was not there; communication between babies in the womb and birth canal, and the women pregnant with them; between twins and triplets in the womb; between a dying woman and the spirit of her incoming grandchild; out-of-body experiences; seeing souls leaving bodies at death; sensing rips and trespassing spirits in a traveller's subtle energy field; past selves' premonitions; a past self's near-death experience; memories of performing sorcery arts; an experience of a dying past self being caught in a 'soul trap' psychically laid by more advanced beings; impressions of other-planet origins; and many others.

A past self saw her friend's past self. A suicidal past self experienced a flashback to a previous life in which he committed suicide — and decided not to kill himself, because it had not solved the problem. A past self burning to death used out-of-body techniques learned in a previous lifetime to lift herself out of agony.

And I have assisted people in an exercise in precognition, to visit lifetimes of their future selves.

FUTURE LIFETIMES
Inner impressions of future lifetimes can be invited through similar techniques to those achieving visits to the past. But in my experience, inner travel to the future has some differences from travel to the past. Information generally arrives more slowly, and involves concepts, thought patterns and events that may shock and confuse the present traveller, as well as stimulate.

A future self may be experienced as an alien being in an alien place, or as, say, a cloud of energy on Earth, able to materialise a pair of human arms for an activity such as sculpting. A future self may perform an operation on his or her own brain.

The future self may not relate to humanoid form, but may relate as a spiritual guide, or perhaps claim to be bio-mechanical — a manufactured biological being.

Future time travel also involves the factor of probability. When is the future *the* future, or a probable future? A personal growth maxim is, 'If you keep on doing what you're doing, you'll end up where you're going.' So, if we change some important attitude, feeling or outlook in the present, what we envisioned as our future is likely to change. Hypnotherapists venture into this territory with a technique applied where a client asks, perhaps, 'Should I have a vasectomy?' The hypnotised client is 'taken into the future' to explore likely effects. So, our probable futures seem also available for viewing.

SPIRITUAL GUIDES

Another avenue of inner exploration is provided by the sensing of inner spiritual guides, which I have mentioned earlier in this book. When people are open to it I make frequent use of this concept, always with beneficial and inspiring results — although immediate discomfort with a spiritual guide figure can occur if the visualised inner figure mirrors closed or hostile behaviour the traveller is unconsciously exhibiting.

American oncologist Dr Carl Simonton and his psychotherapist wife, Stephanie, have made this traditionally mystical concept more accessible since the 1970s, through their life-saving prototypic work around self-awareness with cancer patients. They encourage mental imagery of helpful figures assisting their physical cancer treatments to fight the disease. The guides may appear in human, animal or other form. In teaching seriously ill people to allow this representation of their own inner resources to become available for use, the Simontons have said that relying on such guides assists people to take responsibility for their own health, physically and psychologically.

In past-life work, spiritual guides may be contacted before the journey, to be on call; or after death, to assist with completion processes, or finally to accompany past selves who desire this, on their own journey into the light of higher development.

A spiritual guide can be a source of comfort, clarity, counsel and inspiration uncovered within the traveller. While guides frequently appear on the inner plane as archetypal figures in robes, or as religious characters, a guide may seem to be an angel, a sphere of light, a person known or unknown, an animal, a bird, a geometric shape, or anything else. Spiritual guides can be great assets during a spiritual crisis, which I see as a conflict between old and new orders of consciousness.

COUNTERPART SELVES

Another accessible side road of consciousness is the concept of counterpart selves, about whom little has been written.

Theoretically, these are other human beings on Earth during the same broad time-frame as ourselves, seen as other offshoots from our own soul. The idea is that a mature soul can send several humans to Earth at once, to accelerate the spiritual learning widely seen as the purpose of reincarnation. Such a soul is called an oversoul.

Counterpart selves seem to be psychically available for inner communication. Therapeutically, they are avenues for lessening stress on the present self, and also for tapping more inner resources. Counterpart selves may be of any age, sex or race. They may be alive now or recently dead.

Experimental sessions seem to show that one 'set' of counterpart selves, presumably from the same oversoul, share main life issues but deal with them differently. For example, a counterpart self who is a central American guerilla has spent his life in poverty and is jailed for rebelling against his guerilla leaders when he discovers they are corrupt. The traveller who connects with him feels she has never been able to get enough money, and has continually opposed those teachers and bosses she has seen as inferior.

The work I have begun with this concept, in communication among counterpart selves, has been both mystically challenging and rewarding at the practical level. People who have investigated such connections tell me of ongoing inspiration from their counterpart selves, as well as the development of the ability to disentangle if they wish from the others' emotions and attitudes, which may be exaggerating their own problems. The techniques avoid identification while encouraging understanding.

Counterpart selves do not correspond to the popular image of soulmates. The late consciousness explorer, Jane Roberts, felt that she had met one of her counterpart selves in the flesh — and did not like him!

Nor are they 'parallel selves.' These may be experienced as versions of the self alive in a parallel Universe.

MYTHS AND FAIRYTALES
Another phenomenon of consciousness is that images from myth and fairytale can appear spontaneously in inner vision through past-life work, even sometimes in cartoon form.

In a journey to strengthen my confidence, I 'became' a male giant in a kingdom of tiny people. The images were like storybook illustrations and initially I rejected them as worthless, as imagination.

I was an angry giant, roaring and rampaging around my kingdom, squashing my subjects underfoot — until, on the horizon, appeared a stranger, a female giant. Instantly, a vast joy welled throughout the body of the destructive giant (and my body). He cried, 'Here is my heart!' and wept. The two giants, or parts of myself, married and built roads to avoid stepping on their subjects. That powerful feeling — a giant opening of the heart — is still available to me whenever I recall this simple story. Whether or not it originated in a story I had read as a child is irrelevant. My psyche used it to facilitate change for the better in me.

LEMURIA AND ATLANTIS?
Heart feelings flooded a young woman on a mystical retreat I conducted in outback Australia, at a powerful energy site beside some of the world's oldest rock carvings. After we had recalled past lifetime initiation events, we listened to a taped meditation on the legendary land of Lemuria. Jane was so touched that she cried for an hour.

Lemuria was put forward in the nineteenth century as a possible prehistoric civilisation, a lost continent that sank beneath the ocean 200 000 years ago. The concept developed as an explanation for similarities in flora and fauna of both Africa and India, which would have been linked if such a continent had existed in the Indian Ocean. The idea was taken further by occultists who placed Lemuria in the Pacific Ocean and connected it with Australia. This spurred expeditions on both eastern and western Australian coasts searching for traces of Lemuria, which expedition members believed they found, in Aboriginal art and artifacts.

187

Some occult teachers claim that the Lemurian civilisation evolved beyond our reality, and exists now in an 'etheric', or other-dimensional state, in a form representing a land in a pristine and ideal state of Earthly beauty. I have witnessed a number of spontaneous other-life experiences, unconnected with one another, which seemed to be set in such a land, and featured a race of people who were tall, thin, socially simple, spiritually aware, psychically developed, with their own brand of science. Such experiences have come to people with no conscious knowledge of the stories of Lemuria. Events in those life stories have included death by earthquake, communication with dolphins, scientific experiments with subtle energies. While such events occur in our own time and space, in these stories they were presented through a different kind of mindset, with different lifestyle and social accoutrements.

Jane's powerful impressions beside the ancient carvings in central Australia led her to say, 'I had connected with a part of my essence which appears to be in the energy plane of Lemuria now. I felt such sadness, a deep craving for unity, I longed to be there again!

'In the meditation, I found the place I remember where I was free, where I could teleport at will, where I taught and travelled, sometimes with others, but many times alone. But I was never alone in truth, because I was one with everything. The beauty of that other place was overwhelming. Now I'm grounding this incredible vibration of love.'

Perhaps the legend of an idealised, blissful lifestyle evoked deep grief in Jane over loss of bliss in her current life with other people — or even, possibly, the loss of her 'golden days', her idyllic womb life as an embryo. Releasing grief through the metaphor made room for inspiration.

Numbers of people have discovered life stories in legendary Atlantis that have powerfully affected them. The continent of Atlantis is said to have sunk in the Atlantic Ocean, destroyed by three cataclysms, including man-made nuclear explosion. Some people have been unwilling to tell me they thought they were in Atlantis, because they did not believe in it. (I treat such experiences as potentially valuable in their psychological impact, regardless of historical record.) These stories contained magical feats, different kinds of bodies, archetypal battles between 'good' and 'bad' forces, people arriving on Earth fully formed in a puff of white vapour.

White vapour featured in another story where a woman felt she was a reptile that could jump to the clouds, whose family group worshipped a steam-like substance emitting from rocks. This may represent a mysterious substance studied by three widely diverse mystical groups: alchemists, as the first level of matter; Hindus, as an aid to becoming invisible; and spiritualists, as ectoplasm. Such stories often surprise the people they come to.

MASTERING DEATH?

Some teachers are now de-throning death, saying that perhaps death is only a habit. This idea appears in ancient scriptures. The great Indian sage, Shankara, wrote of it, 'People grow old and die because they see other people grow old and die.' What if we actually have a choice — whether to continue reincarnating, or to choose to master the physical body we now have and become physically immortal?

Remember the quantum science discoveries, that matter — the body — is not solid, but is a bonding of subatomic particles of trapped light, vibrating in a frequency pattern we call 'body'. Rather than discarding a level of our energy every time we die, might we aim at claiming all of it?

'Spiritualising' matter means to raise the frequency of its vibrational rate to evolve beyond the frequencies of entropy and decay, through raising consciousness. Mastering the body would mean that we would be able to heal it, change it, levitate it, transport it anywhere by intention alone, and thus enjoy Earth life to the full for as long as we wished. Physical Immortalist literature from ancient scriptures implies that such individuals can also consciously exist in other dimensions. Astounding abilities already developed by evolving humans are on record as eventually becoming familiar in their daily lives. St Teresa of Avila is documented as finding levitating a nuisance when she was busy. St Joseph of Cupertino was discouraged from waiting at table in case he levitated with the dishes.

In rejecting 'deathist' attitudes, Physical Immortalists point out that many major religions have their traditions of individuals demonstrating such mastery, including Christian and Jewish. Biographies of more than 1000 Taoist Immortals were published in China in 1726. Hinduism, Shintoism and others feature stories of Immortals.

The mystic poet and Immortalist teacher Robert Coon says of the connections between spirituality and the body: 'Generating praise, joy and gratitude for the divine sets off a resonance at atomic levels, and your body begins to unify itself. When our collective spirituality has reached a certain level, there'll be a big shift in planetary evolution.

'We can't get there through fear of death, we have to heal that. Ageing is accumulated over many decades of minor ingratitudes that build up at cellular level. The radiance of thanksgiving is the best thing you can put out, it dissolves the issue !

'The Immortals' datebook is in centuries, you've got all the time in the world.'

Forecasting for the far future an immortal planet where everyone is immortal, Robert Coon believes that everyone is on this pathway, 'but in which incarnation is personal choice. We're all experts at dying. Why not try something new?'

If you had a choice — whether to die, or instead to master Earth conditions, how might you choose?

UFO ABDUCTION STORIES

Another mind-boggling phenomenon that cannot be explained is being taken with growing seriousness by some psychotherapists and psychiatrists. This is the increasing number of widespread reports of abduction of humans by several forms of aliens, usually involving a UFO, and now sometimes also involving past lifetime stories.

Therapists have become involved because of excessive stress exhibited by people who feel they have had that experience, usually not just once but many times. They live in terror, never knowing when it will happen next.

Thousands of people are admitting to such memories. They tell of being paralysed and helpless against alien intention while nearby family members seem to be made unconscious; of being 'floated', or levitated, through walls and air into a craft where they are subjected to physical examination and interference that can be painful. People reporting abduction events tend to place them on the borderline between tangible reality and inner experience. Some show, as 'evidence', physical scarring which they claim appeared overnight.

Many say they have been physically experimented on or forced into sexual activity with other humans or aliens. Men say they have had sperm taken. Women tell of being implanted during abduction with hybrid foetuses which are removed during abduction three months afterwards — causing the pregnancies to be classed as phantom pregnancies — then of later being abducted to meet strange hybrid children in UFOs.

A Harvard professor of psychiatry, Dr John Mack, has written one of the most comprehensive books relating personal accounts of a number of people who tell of such abduction in detail. Dr Mack cites experiences told by those abducted that involve one or more of their past lives.

He recounts how one woman recalled aliens in a UFO showing her, on a screen, scenes they told her were from one of her past lives. She immediately identified with this story in overpowering sensation through re-living emotional scenes, and drew from it a helpful message relating to her current life. Other patients were shown lifetimes in which the self had tried to better the human condition, or in which the self had had alien contact and/or been abducted by aliens. The past lifetime input was apparently part of indoctrination programs those abducted received from aliens, saying that Earth is escalating major physical cataclysms as the planet self-destructs because of humanity's polluting practices. One of those abducted wondered, 'Do humans hate their future so much they'll destroy it?'

Dr Mack, a former Freudian analyst, comments on the role of past lives in the spiritual growth exhibited by some of these people in his study. He writes that one value of past-life experiences is that it puts a different perspective on the nature of human identity, pointing out the smallness of an individual lifetime from a cosmic perspective. Viewing one's personal growth as a continuing path over more than one lifetime, he feels, is especially strengthening.

Initially challenged by his Harvard colleagues on his abduction work, Dr Mack was subsequently asked by those colleagues to form a working party to investigate anomalous phenomena generally. He has since worked with indigenous American and African abductees, and others in several countries. Dr Mack is one of a number of observers who see potential for self-transformation in such accounts, which have been mapped by other transpersonal researchers in recent years.

A number of top scientists believe our galaxy contains at least 10 000 other civilisations among the 400 billion planets in the Milky Way. Cosmologists began searching for intelligent signals from the universe in the 'sixties, in a program of radio frequency sweeps called SETI (Search for Extra Terrestial Intelligence). Based in the U.S., SETI employed radiotelescope time at the astronomy station at Parkes, New South Wales. The search escalated as instruments became more powerful. Over 35 years, 35 significant signals have been received, but none repeated.

So it may be illogical to totally discount people's accounts of meeting, or even of having been, aliens. Aliens may even be native to Earth, but at home in other dimensions. If the universe is, as astronomer Sir James Jeans suggested, a giant thought rather than a giant machine, then the universe as a vast range of consciousness holds phenomena unrecognised by humanity.

Research, including my own on UFO/alien reports, shows that, not uncommonly, experiences of sightings, contact and violation have been accompanied by stress-related illness, depression, breakdown, dislike of being touched and inability to be sexually intimate. I find rebirthing sessions powerful in releasing such stresses.

But death, apparently premature, is also a factor in some cases. Some of my clients have recalled UFO contact in previous lives as well as in this life, including an experience that killed a past self.

AN EVOLUTIONARY SELF?

Not all UFO stories involve violation. A woman who thought she had an open mind sought her first incarnation on Earth. But when she found that the self contacted lived in a UFO and wore a white jumpsuit, she wanted to stop the regression because it seemed like a science-fiction movie.

This self, Arunna, insisted that he was an advanced version of the traveller, who had changed dimensions. He had then revisited Earth back at a time of its cooling, millions of years ago, in an area covered by great volcanoes caused by violent displacement of tectonic plates. He said his visit was a rescue expedition to repair Earth's electromagnetic field so that the planet could harbour the future we now experience.

This past-and-future self described himself as a multi-dimensional being, a cosmic explorer taking a human form

192

when on Earth, adopting other physical bodies in other places, living in 'a body of consciousness' on his home planet. Therefore he was — is — immortal, and still learning, in particular learning how to manipulate consciousness. He mentioned a training class held 'in the wilds of deep space' where each (embodied) class member had had to leave the craft and manifest solid substance in space to walk on.

Regression: Our consciousness is broader than yours, our emotions have stabilised. Barriers you are currently dealing with have dissolved for us. There is no guilt to your having erected those barriers. It is a natural part of evolution and you are dissolving them bit by bit. Earth is one of many training grounds for the developing consciousness.

I have been to Earth in four ages on expeditions to correct different imbalances in Nature. In the time of the volcanoes my physical body moved around safely on the hot ground on cushions of air. We understand these bodies, so they don't need to get ill or be damaged.

At another time of endless rain, I learned to fly the body above trees to repair atmospheric imbalances.

These activities correlate metaphysically to higher energies. Healing done in one realm reaches to another in another form, and again, like a hall of mirrors.

To adjust planetary energies among the volcanoes, we worked with a giant crystal in the ship. It had been mathematically accelerated, following the principle of life-expansion forever. The cosmos is like the crystal, multi-faceted. Your universe is one little facet, our universe is another.

We came on our expeditions because of love and interest. There are many avenues to express love in the cosmos.

Well, the more we explore past lifetimes, the more doors open up within consciousness, within our reality. The Sufis have a saying, 'Beware of the man who knows.' The search for knowledge seems open-ended and never-ending, certainly in an age where the old world view is rapidly changing. New ideas disturb our comfort zones. As old certainties crumble, as we send out vehicles and instruments to probe a galaxy that contains conditions of time, space and consciousness that could blow our minds, the human race is poised on the edge of possibility.

In personal terms, this means that what was once thought impossible may not be — including reincarnation. Yet, true or not, past lifetimes are not mere curiosities 'back there'. Their energies live in our present and affect our consciousness, hindering or empowering us. Through life story therapy we can meet our past selves, learn from them, help them heal and develop.

By doing this, we accelerate our own progress into an exciting, expanding state of being: the state of becoming all that we can be.

MY PAST LIFETIMES COUNSELLING TECHNIQUES

I am not a typical past lifetimes practitioner — if there is such a person. Some of the approaches described below break new ground.

In one sense they de-mystify because, in my experience, past lifetime impressions are often easily accessible to people, who then realise that traces of past selves have been familiar all their lives.

My personal growth approaches respect the normal impetus of the individual towards self-healing. While the techniques are apparently simple, they access natural, non-ordinary states of consciousness in which people can finish negative karma by transforming it into positive.

I see five areas that involve ideas new to many people.

1. *Belief in reincarnation is unnecessary.* Benefits do not depend on belief. My aim is to support the client to feel whatever he or she needs to feel, in order to heal old emotional pain and release old negative conditioning. In that sense, when I write of 'healing past lifetimes', I mean facing, feeling and resolving current personal issues, in past lifetime form. This demonstrably creates change for the better in the present moment.

2. *Hypnosis is only one option.* While many past lifetime practitioner/authors use hypnosis, I seldom do. Although I qualified as a clinical hypnotherapist in New South Wales in 1984, and I consider hypnosis an excellent tool, around that time I also discovered the work of Californian therapist Dr Morris Netherton, who preferred non-hypnotic techniques to induce past lifetimes regression. This is a basis I have extended.

A 1994 review of the current past lifetimes field through the work of some major practitioners in America reported results both with and without hypnosis. This review appeared in the award-winning *New Age Journal.*

One conclusion was that past lifetimes therapy is psycho-spiritual in nature: within the practice, we deal with sacred dimensions of our everyday life. The review reported that increasing numbers of people who have undertaken this psycho-spiritual work tell of healings of many kinds, from lifelong fear of drowning, to severe asthma, to suicidal tendencies, to relationship problems — sometimes achieved in one consultation, as also quoted in this book.

3. *Reliving alone is not necessarily enough.* I believe that the relief and insights obtained by simple reliving of the past-life are often only the beginning of the self-improvement available. I accelerate the immediate completion of destructive karmic issues through involving past-life characters in simple techniques. These include processes on truth-telling, anger and forgiveness. And trauma release is a vital element.

4. *Past-life resolution is a vibrational activity.* I approach past-life work in the light of new scientific developments, such as field-of-energy medicine. US physician Dr Richard Gerber includes past lifetimes therapy in a leading edge survey of energy healing modalities he predicts will comprise a major option in 21st century healthcare, affecting mind, emotions, body and spirit. Energetics medicine, or vibrational medicine, involves what he calls higher dimensional anatomy, that is, the human subtle energy field traditionally called the aura, which has now been verified by scientific instruments and studies.

5. *A breathing technique activates memories.* It is not generally known that for many people, past lifetime memories are only a few breaths away.

A primary method I employ to contact and resolve issues through past lifetime awareness is an amazing breathing technique called rebirthing, or breathwork, a 20-year-old revival of a sustained-breathing meditational practice used within ancient spiritual traditions in the East.

Rebirthing sessions are conducted by qualified rebirthing practitioners, who not only have been educated in this non-drug, self-discovery technique, but also use it themselves for stress release, health maintenance, personal and spiritual growth. Rebirthing was named by American seminar leader Leonard Orr who discovered and developed it in the 'seventies, after he spontaneously experienced birth recall.

Various streams of rebirthing, or breathwork, deal differently with emotions. The-in depth approach I support is to accept and 'heal', or evolve, uncomfortable emotions, rather than to focus on consciously dropping them.

Breathwork is profound. It reveals an unsuspected interface of breath, birth and past lifetime impressions, which has proved safe. As breathwork is now practised in the United States, Australia, England, Russia, Scandanavia, Germany, Poland, and other parts of Europe, Africa, Singapore, New Zealand and other countries, countless people are now spontaneously contacting other-life impressions by simply breathing in a continuous pattern — whether or not they believe in reincarnation.

SCIENTIFIC BASIS

Scientific understanding of connections between breathwork and non-ordinary consciousness phenomena are described in a number of books by the American psychiatrist Dr Stanislav Grof, former Chief of Psychiatric Research at the Maryland Psychiatric Research Centre, and a former Professor of Psychiatry at Johns Hopkins University School of Medicine. His research provides a practical and conceptual framework for otherwise apparently inexplicable results from the breathing technique which is now a basis of his work.

In three decades of original research, resulting in a new map of consciousness, Dr Grof has studied the emergence and therapeutic effects of spontaneous birth — and past lifetime — memories, as part of a spectrum of inner experiences he first observed in LSD therapy. When LSD was banned, Dr Grof discovered that people could obtain similar therapeutic experiences through a pattern of sustained breathing. He calls his breathwork style 'holotropic therapy'.

PROFOUND EXPERIENCES

I came to this work through my own life challenges, including divorce trauma, near-death experience, and spiritual emergency. In my early rebirthing sessions in 1984 in New South Wales, I began going through profound spontaneous experiences of what appeared to be several past lifetimes, during my basic training as a rebirther. Through the powerful healing effects of these on my own outlook and life, I realised the value of such recall, which continued through subsequent training courses in transpersonal studies and consciousness research.

197

I then studied the work of major past lifetime therapists and developed my system of past lifetimes counselling, as a modality separate to, yet overlapping, rebirthing. As a past-lifetimes counsellor, I continue to study past-life recall both through my ongoing consultancy as a transpersonal practitioner and trainer, and through my own spiritual practices.

Rebirthing sessions also stimulated a New York Jungian psychotherapist, Dr Roger Woolger, to explore past lifetimes, as he records in his book *Other Lives, Other Selves*. His first breathwork session inspired his comment that new dimensions of the nature of both personality and mental illness had opened up for him through his breath.

But past lifetimes practitioners generally are unlikely to adopt breathwork, which requires training in its own right — firstly, because it does not trigger past-lifetimes impressions for everyone, and so does not reliably allow 'dialling' of past lifetimes specific to a present aim; secondly, because other experiences it triggers are generally outside the relevance of past lifetimes counselling. (Over a series of breathwork sessions, these may include biographical memories from the breather's current life, all the way back to, and often including, birth or womb experience, as well as visionary spiritual connections to nature, Earth, the cosmos, archetypal and Creator energies.)

The stream of rebirthing I am qualified to use is named 'transpersonal rebirthing' (a registered Trade Mark of the Living Water Centre, NSW, founded by Ahrara Bhakti.) This style is influenced by the scientific findings and breathwork approach of Dr Grof, and also derives from the rebirthing research of Leonard Orr. A session is initially focused on a present-life issue, but is non-directive and non-intrusive. It incorporates music, can allow emotional release through sound and movement, includes supportive bodywork and guiding techniques if needed.

Past lifetime exploration in a breath session is dealt with in the moment: ideally, the rebirther does not guide the client to explore the story, but to identify where the spontaneous past lifetime trace is being acted out in the present lifetime.

Because my studies have led me to see valuable opportunities for in-depth use of the memories, I may suggest that a client contacting past lifetime impressions in a rebirthing session could later have sessions in guided past lifetimes counselling. Through past-life impressions, I then apply personal growth techniques to access insights, choices and changes at a level of consciousness not normally available.

With or without initial contact through rebirthing, I find that usually three past lifetime sessions allow basic resolution of problems, attitudinal change, and/or retrieval of buried personal strengths. Subsequent sessions deepen and expand these benefits.

After a session, the client and I share what the discoveries may mean for the client's present life. In keeping with emerging clinical attitudes supporting the client's self-responsibility, I prefer to serve as a facilitator rather than to dominate through the old-style paradigm of expert-and-patient.

IMPRESSION RETRIEVAL METHODS

Here is a broad outline of ways I use to guide people to contact past lifetimes impressions:

Rebirthing. A person lies comfortably, eyes closed, breathing without pauses. I prefer breathing to be sustained for up to an hour and a half. As this style of breath meditation requires 'mindfulness', or conscious awareness, a breather may notice spontaneous body sensations, impressions, images, feelings, insights, memories of the current life, or also of other lives. The breath pattern accesses deeper states of consciousness.

In a session, a person's current feeling of being 'weighed down' by problems may trigger impressions of a body in a past lifetime being literally weighed or weighted down, and also similar impressions of constriction and heaviness felt during his or her birth journey into this life. Continual breathing automatically releases the chain of related pressures, as the rebirther supports the breather to move through any difficult tensions towards their permanent release.

Dream exploration. A person recalls a dream, and is guided to discover, explore and resolve its significances. The dream may seem to be of events experienced by another person — perhaps a past self — or may lead into this.

Association. When a client speaks of his or her current life experiences in metaphor or simile, I encourage exploration of such phrases, seemingly used by chance but often vital clues to some unresolved past lifetime situation that can be seen to be influencing the present. For example, 'What she said to me felt like a knife going through me' may lead to an inner vision of a swordfight in another self's time and place. The unresolved issues of that self are being played out in the present life of the speaker, concerning, say, unfounded accusations of blame, that originally led to death. A willingness to recognise such gifts from the unconscious allows a client to utilise them to work through present feelings of conflict. In this case the story possibly involves anger, misunderstandings, and a current out-of-proportion sense of being in danger now.

Body feedback. I also use the above approach in cases of physical stress symptoms, asking, 'And this feels as if...?' 'It feels as if there is a hole in my stomach' may hold the seed of a useful story.

Belief system identification. A client and I identify the basic stress response in his or her current situation, perhaps a feeling of 'I'm not good enough.' The client then continues to repeat, 'When I feel not good enough, I feel as if...' Repetition may evoke impressions developing into a previously unknown story.
  Or I may suggest that the client 'goes back to where this belief began'. The client may identify a causal point in the current life. Behind this, however, will be a past-life source, possibly rooted in trauma which can then be cleared, thus lessening the emotional energy maintaining the belief.

Reiki (a Japanese word meaning the application of universal life force). This now widespread system of touch healing can stimulate spontaneous past lifetime impressions in the course of releasing stress. As an attuned Reiki practitioner, I may regard recall by a client receiving my touch as all that needs to happen in a particular case. Or I may suggest following up with a past lifetimes counselling session for in-depth exploration and further resolution.

Discussion. In groups or one-to-one, exchanging ideas and experiences concerning either reincarnation or other-life recall can reduce anxiety about such exploration, so that past lifetimes recall is stimulated, even for the first time.

Meditation. A simple guided meditation to a beautiful place in Nature and along a path can lead a client to the consciousness realm of past lifetime memory. This is illustrated by the large number of such meditation tapes that have become available to people wishing to explore their own minds, since past-life work has been recognised as an important, if optional, aspect of the personal growth field.

Hypnosis. As past lifetime memories reside so close to awareness that they can be subsequently recognisable in our everyday attitudes, feelings, even words, I usually do not find hypnosis necessary. However, in particular cases, it is extremely useful, for example, where people acknowledge that they are prejudiced against reincarnational memories yet are willing to try anything to improve their quality of life.

Other techniques. I sometimes use other potential amplifiers of distant memory, such as psychodrama, sound, or body feedback.

BIBLIOGRAPHY

Reference Sources:

Fritjof Capra *The Turning Point* Flamingo,1982

Joan Frances Casey with Lynn Wilson *The Flock: the Autobiography of a Multiple Personality* Fawcett Columbine, 1991

Gina Cerminara *Many Mansions* Signet, 1978

Robert Coon *Physical Immortality: History, Theory and Techniques* A.A. Avalon, 1989

Encyclopedia of Religion Ed. in Chief: Mircea Eliade, Macmillan Publishing Co.,1987

Marilyn Ferguson *Aquarius Now* J P Tarcher, 1994

Russell Freedman & James E. Morriss *The Brains of Animals and Man* Holiday House Inc., 1972

Edith Fiore *Abduction : Encounters with Extra Terrestials* Sidgwick & Jackson, 1989

Edith Fiore *You Have Been Here Before* Ballantine, 1978

George Gallup Jnr. *Adventures in Immortality* McGraw Hill, 1982

Richard Gerber *Vibrational Medicine* Bear & Co.,1988

Bruce Goldberg *Past Lives, Future Lives* Newcastle, 1982

Christina Groff & Stanislav Groff *The Stormy Search for the Self: Understanding and Living with Spiritual Emergency* Mandala 1991

Stanislav Grof *Beyond the Brain* State University of New York Press,1985
Stanislav Grof *The Adventure of Self Discovery* State University of New York Press, 1988

Stanislav Grof with Hal Zina Bennett *The Holotropic Mind* Harper, 1992

Ed. Stanislav & Christina Grof *Spiritual Emergency* J. P .Tarcher, 1989

Arthur Guirdham *A Foot in Both Worlds* Neville Spearman, 1973

Arthur Guirdham *We Are One Another* Neville Spearman, 1974

Arthur Guirdham *The Great Heresy* Neville Spearman, 1977

Louise L. Hay *You Can Heal Your Life* Hay House, 1984

Frederick Leboyer *Birth Without Violence* Fontana/Collins, 1977

John E. Mack *Abduction : Human Encounters with Aliens* Simon & Schuster, 1994

Bob Mandel *Two Hearts are Better Than One* Celestial Arts, 1988

Bob Mandel *Open Heart Therapy* Celestial Arts, 1986

Morris Netherton & Nancy Shiftin *Past Life Therapy* Compendium, 1978

Michel Odent *Primal Health* Century, 1986

Mark Pearson *From Healing to Awakening* Inner Work Partnership, 1991

Sondra Ray & Bob Mandel *Birth and Relationships* Celestial Arts, 1987

Sondra Ray *Celebration of Breath* Celestial Arts, 1983

Sondra Ray *Loving Relationships* Celestial Arts, 1980

Steve Richards *Invisibility* Aquarian Press, 1982

Marge Rieder *Mission to Millboro* Blue Dolphin Pub. Co., 1993

Kenneth Ring *Heading Towards Omega* Quill, 1984

Adriana Rocha & Kristi Jorde *A Child of Eternity,* Piatkus, 1995

Peter Russell *The Global Brain* J. P. Tarcher, 1983

Rupert Sheldrake *A New Science of Life* Blond & Briggs, 1984

Rupert Sheldrake *The Presence of the Past* Collins, 1988

Carl Simonton, Stephanie Matthews-Simonton, James L. Creighton *Getting Well Again,* J. P. Tarcher, 1978

Hal Stone & Sidra Winkelman *Embracing Our Selves* De Vorss & Co., 1985

Dick Sutphen *You Were Born Again To be Together* Pocket Books, 1976

Michael Talbot *The Holographic Universe* Grafton Books, 1991

The Higher Taste Bhaktivedanta Book Trust, 1983

Ena Twigg with Ruth Hagy Brod *Ena Twigg: Medium* Manor Books, 1973

Thomas Verny with John Kelly *The Secret Life of the Unborn Child* Sphere, 1982

Helen Wambach *Reliving Past Lives* Barnes & Noble, 1978

Dr Joel Whitton & Joe Fisher *Life Between Life* Grafton, 1987

Roger Woolger *Other Lives, Other Selves* Doubleday, 1987

Paramahansa Yogananda *Autobiography of a Yogi* Rider for Self-Realisation Fellowship, 1950

JOURNALS

'Exploring the implications of the freezing phenomenon', Sykes J. & Sykes D., *International Journal for Past Lifetimes*

Research and Therapy, Vol. 1, January 1982

Interview with Ngakpa Chogyam Rinpoche, *Association for Transpersonal Psychology Newsletter,* USA, Spring 1994

'Reincarnation and the Taj Mahal', Dr Gladys McGarey, *Healing Currents,* Journal of the Whole Health Institute, USA, Winter 1993

'Remembrances of Lives Past', *New Age Journal,* US, November 1994

'Human Origins: A Family Feud', *New Scientist,* May 20, 1995.

TAPES

Consciousness and the Unfolding Universe, Professor David Bohm, Wrekin Trading Company, England

LAZARIS tapes, Concept Synergy, USA

Visions of Hope, Michaelmas Trust, England

TELEVISION PROGRAM

AUSTRALIA: Channel 2 *Lateline: Final Frontier,* broadcast 15 February, 1995

DO YOU HAVE AN EXPERIENCE TO SHARE?

Please send (typed) any relevant experiences to author
Annie O'Grady
C/- Sally Milner Publishing
RMB 54 Burra Road
Burra Creek, NSW Australia 2620

PERSONAL AND TRANSPERSONAL DEVELOPMENT

Transpersonal counselling in its many forms guides people to use
any personal challenge as a catalyst to release larger life potentials, through expanding spiritual and metaphysical dimensions
of experience.

TRAININGS (experiential), CONSULTATIONS, RETREATS,
INTENSIVES

Annie O'Grady
Adelaide Hills, South Australia
Australia 5152
Tel/Fax 08 8370 9139

Self-help audiotape available:
'Visit a Past Lifetime You've Shared with
Someone You Know Now'

THE AUSTRALIAN SPIRITUAL EMERGENCE NETWORK,
a referral and education service for people in
transformational crisis, may be reach through contact person
Paul Perfrement
40 Moyran Parade
Grays Point, NSW 2232
Telephone (02) 9526 8363

ABOUT THE AUTHOR

Annie O'Grady is a personal growth consultant. For fourteen years she has been guiding people around Australia from many backgrounds to create change for the better in their lives.

A former adventure novelist, radio playwright and journalist, Annie decided to train in self-transformation techniques that had helped her through a marriage break-up and identity crisis.

A near-death experience through illness had led Annie to learn to apply spiritual experiences to release material problems. This spurred a deep interest in exploring holistic healthcare, and hidden realms of consciousness.

Past Lifetimes: Keys for Change comes out of her work with clients and students in practical metaphysical studies, particularly in past lifetimes resolution, transpersonal rebirthing and dream exploration.